History of Brazil

An Enthralling Guide to Ancient Indigenous Civilizations, Portuguese Colonization, the Imperial Era, and Modern Times

Free limited time bonus

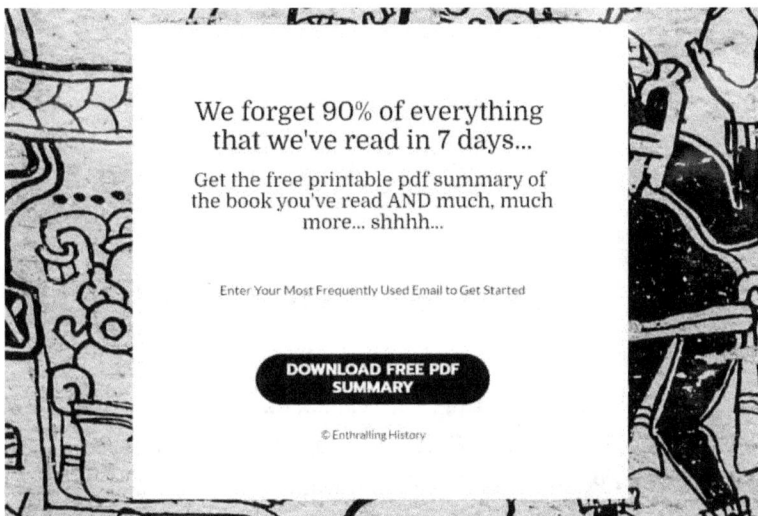

We forget 90% of everything
that we've read in 7 days...

Get the free printable pdf summary of
the book you've read AND much, much
more... shhhh...

Enter Your Most Frequently Used Email to Get Started

**DOWNLOAD FREE PDF
SUMMARY**

© Enthralling History

Stop for a moment. We have a free bonus set up for you. The problem is this: we forget 90% of everything that we read after 7 days. Crazy fact, right? Here's the solution: we've created a printable, 1-page pdf summary for this book that you're reading now. All you have to do to get your free pdf summary is to go to the following website: https://livetolearn.lpages.co/enthrallinghistory/

Or, Scan the QR code!

Once you do, it will be intuitive. Enjoy, and thank you!

Table of Contents

Introduction

Brazil boasts a uniquely vibrant culture, an eclectic mix of people from diverse social or ethnic backgrounds, and a rich and vast natural landscape. As one of the largest countries in the world and one of the most important politically, it is naturally very interesting to examine how it got there. How did Brazil become such a particularly remarkable country? Which developments led to one nation controlling such a huge chunk of land, full of surprises and secrets—some of which we are still unsure about? Who were some of the most important figures who shaped what Brazil is today?

The answers to these and many more questions about Brazil lie in the nation's history, which is very compelling to examine. It is a combination of dynamic and memorable events that capture the curiosity of people of all kinds, whether familiar with the broader context in which the history of Brazil must be placed or simply interested in finding out more about a country they love. Brazilian history certainly contains something for everyone and is full of occurrences that coincide with other social and historical circumstances around the world. This is true for both the pre- and post-Columbian eras, though we know far less about the former than about the latter.

The centuries-long struggle of the Brazilian people, which continues even today, is not just marked by their adverse relations with foreign conquerors and colonizers. One of the main struggles of the Brazilian people, including the Indigenous population and those who settled the nation after the arrival of Portuguese colonizers, was with European ideas. Much like in other colonies in the Americas and around the world, efforts to Europeanize Brazil were prevalent. The colonizers brought a distinct set of ideas, attitudes, practices, and traditions, and their diffusion from Europe to Brazil accelerated during the eighteenth and nineteenth centuries.

European institutions and ways of thought were challenged by the Indigenous and African populations of Brazil, whose lives had been drastically affected by the age of European colonization. It can be argued that Brazil, the country as we know it today, was born only after these cultures synthesized with European culture. As we will see, they exerted their own influence on the colonizers, a process that culminated with the independence of Brazil in 1822—an event that transformed the socio-political landscape of the Western Hemisphere and affected the European power struggles in the "Old World."

Thus, it is interesting to closely examine Brazil's history and think about the most important developments that greatly influenced Brazil's evolution into its present form. A good way to do this is to look at Brazil's past in the wider context of the European colonization of the Americas, though even here Brazil stands out as a unique example because of its Portuguese origins in contrast to Spanish or Anglo-Franco America. Nevertheless, as a European colony, Brazil shared many experiences with struggling Latin and North American nations, most of which achieved their independence in the nineteenth century. In this regard, Brazilian history is a narrative of its people's efforts to assert universal liberties and shape their own destiny and path to progress.

And yet, despite having overthrown the yoke of the Europeans in 1822, the last two hundred years of Brazilian history have been marked by just as much political and socio-economic turmoil. The post-colonial legacy can still be observed in Brazil, as in most, if not all, post-colonial societies. One aspect of Brazilian life today that instantly comes to mind as a clear result of centuries of colonial meddling is the country's diverse ethnocultural makeup. Brazil is a melting pot of Indigenous American, European, and African populations. It also is one of the primary examples of a society where all these different groups managed to integrate seamlessly.

Still, ironically, the main challenges Brazil faces today can be compared to those it faced hundreds of years earlier. Despite the country's significant territorial possessions and vast resources, it is plagued with high levels of social and economic inequality. In the twentieth century, the country underwent significant political changes, including a lengthy military dictatorship, which damaged the integrity of its political structure. To this day, many are skeptical of the country's political and economic elites because of widespread corruption, which also penetrates Brazilian civil services. Ultimately, the problems that shape Brazil today are multifold, and the only way to properly address them is to examine the historical circumstances in which they arose.

Thus, this book offers a concise history of Brazil. In the opening chapters, we will briefly examine the Indigenous societies that dwelled in Brazil before the arrival of European colonizers in the Americas in the late fifteenth century. Unfortunately, our knowledge of this era is mostly limited to European sources and the archeological legacy that remains, which means there is still much more to know about Indigenous Brazilians.

Then, we will move on to the history of Brazil as a colony, from a Portuguese enclave in a Spanish-dominated New World to the largest country in South America. We will examine the economic, political, cultural, and social factors that contributed to the development of Portuguese Brazil. This era laid the foundations of what Brazil would become once it attained independence from the colonizers. We will look at the struggle for independence that transformed the political landscape of Brazil and the entire Western Hemisphere. Finally, the book will tell the story of Brazil's violent and tumultuous shift to democracy from imperialism and the challenges the country had to face since the late nineteenth century. Likewise, we will examine the modern importance of Brazil in Latin American and international political affairs.

Chapter One – The Origins of Colonial Brazil

Age of Exploration

The Late Middle Ages, lasting from roughly the fourteenth to the sixteenth centuries, was a pivotal time in European history—and for good reasons. Politically, the Europeans had managed to reach a somewhat stable status quo, especially in comparison to the previous millennium or so after the fall of Rome in 476. Most kingdoms, such as England or France, had already defined their borders with each other and had established a Christian order with a distinguished social system. They saw the pope as the de facto leader of the Christian world. The expansion of Islam, which had been perhaps the greatest perceived threat to European stability, had mostly been contained.

With the advent of the Ottoman Empire and the fall of Constantinople in 1453, the situation in Europe began to change. Catholic Europe saw an influx of migrants from the former lands of the Byzantine Empire now under the control of the Ottomans. Various scholars, nobles, merchants, and members of the Christian clergy moved to Europe, bringing valuable possessions that included manuscripts of classical antiquity, preserved in the vaults of Greek Churches and previously inaccessible to Western Europeans. This resulted in the renewed will to learn and rediscover the rich classical past of Europe, lost with the chaos that had ensued since the fall of the Western Roman Empire.

This new movement, at first practiced by the richer members of Italian society, would become known as the Renaissance, or "rebirth." The Renaissance, one of the most fundamental products of medieval European thought, was not only concerned with art, literature, and architecture. It also resulted in the development of humanism—a movement that attributed more importance to the capabilities of humans as rational actors who could shape the world they lived in.

In turn, Europeans slowly but surely began studying the world they inhabited. Even as Christianity retained its importance as the chief guide to ordering European life, the humanist movement of the Renaissance made late medieval Europeans hungry for knowledge and understanding. Ironically, the Catholic status quo would eventually be challenged by the Europeans, now increasingly educated in arts, humanities, philosophy, and science. Before the Scientific Revolution of the late sixteenth century and the later Enlightenment movement fundamentally shook up the technological and moral foundations of the continent, however, another development had more immediate material consequences for European kingdoms. It was the beginning of the Age of Exploration.

During the Age of Exploration, also called the Age of Discovery, European nations increasingly undertook more daring voyages, trying to explore what lay beyond the borders of their continent. In hindsight, one might find it strange that the extent of Europe's knowledge of the world was very limited back then. Yes, they knew of faraway places like China and India, having traded with them through intermediary merchants for centuries. Their knowledge of Africa, on the other hand, was mostly limited to the northern coast. From old and new stories, Europe had a rough idea of these distant lands, which it knew produced some of the most valuable materials. Yet, these accounts were often unreliable. In addition, it only became possible to explore the world as the scientific developments of the Renaissance years began to revolutionize navigation and shipbuilding.

At the forefront of European exploration was the Kingdom of Portugal, which began its overseas expansion at the beginning of the fifteenth century. Several factors allowed the Portuguese to undertake such endeavors—circumstances that were simply not true for other Europeans that early. One such factor was Portugal's political landscape at that time, which was very stable and marked with fewer complications. Of course, we must consider that Portugal as a kingdom had been formed after hundreds of years of war against the Muslim dominions of Iberia, which had emerged in the peninsula after the initial stage of Islamic expansion in the eighth century. Portugal was established during the Reconquista, the effort of Christian kings to reclaim Iberia. Since its emergence as an independent kingdom in the twelfth century, Portugal had expanded its territories at the expense of not only Muslims but also neighboring Christian kingdoms. In the late fourteenth century, the kingdom finally cemented its position, with borders close to its modern ones after King John I (Dom João I) became the first ruler of the new Joanine dynasty or House of Aviz.

In fact, the Portuguese policy of overseas expansion was directly influenced by the circumstances created after the monarchy's centralization under the House of Aviz. Different forces began to gain power and influence in the royal court, and all had their own interests and designs for exploration. The monarchy saw overseas expansion as a pragmatic way of boosting the kingdom's income after years of constant wars had significantly depleted the treasury.

Personal enrichment was also the main motivation behind the rising merchant class—a relatively new social class that had emerged as a vital part of Portuguese society.

The Catholic Church, on the other hand, believed that expansion provided an avenue for further spreading God's word and its mission to "heathen" societies. This was especially important for the Portuguese Catholic Church because its history had been shaped by fighting against non-Christian forces.

A lot of commoners were also eager to jump on expeditionary ships and be the first ones into the unknown. For them, especially the male population, it meant the prospect of a new beginning, perhaps one that promised great wealth for those who dared to go on such journeys.

The only major sector of society that was less keen on investing in overseas expansion was the landowning nobility. The nobles enjoyed the status quo and believed that the outpouring of more people in search of new lands to conquer, trading routes to monopolize, and heathens to Christianize acted as a detriment to the labor force on their estates.

The socio-political state of Portugal was thus very important when it came to the early efforts to explore beyond the known parts of the world. However, there were other "enablers" of Portugal's jumpstart in its colonial and expeditionary endeavors.

First, as we mentioned earlier, technological developments in seafaring and navigation allowed for longer and riskier voyages on the high seas. Since the 1440s, the Portuguese increasingly began to use the new caravel ships that were highly mobile and designed to sail in shallow waters, as well. Prince Henry the Navigator (1394-1460), the fourth child of Dom João I whose nickname suggests his active involvement in expeditionary affairs, played a big part. He sponsored many of the initial voyages in exchange

Henry the Navigator.[1]

for a percentage of the profits the expedition would make. Prince Henry believed that the future of Portugal lay overseas, in whatever form it may have come, partially because the Reconquista had been already completed.

Overseas expansion was thus perceived as a legitimate way of expanding Portuguese economic and political power. There was also a wider need to find new trade routes to Asia—Europe's longtime supplier of valuable trade materials, especially spices and silk. The expansion of the Ottoman Empire resulted in the monopolization of trade routes by Ottoman merchants, who had close ties with Genoese and Venetian traders. This resulted in the Italians getting a lion's share of the profit by dominating Mediterranean trade coming from the Ottoman Empire. This also contributed to the high level of development of Italian states during the Late Middle Ages.

Before Portugal reached Brazil, however, or even before such long-distance voyages were even perceived to be possible, Portuguese overseas activities were mostly confined to the West African coast. Throughout the fifteenth century, Portuguese expeditions made their way south along the African coast, reaching Cape Bojador in 1434 and, crucially, the Cape of Good Hope in 1487. They did not bother to travel deep into the African continent but instead stuck close to the shore, setting up several trading forts with a permanent small military presence. This meant the Portuguese had a head start in profiting from the goods that flowed out from this part of Africa, most importantly ivory and gold dust.

The Portuguese also held the Atlantic islands close to Europe and Western Africa—Madeira, the Azores, Cape Verde, and São Tomé, which were all acquired throughout the fifteenth century. These islands acted as a reliable network for expanding and concentrating Portuguese trading activities. Each was developed economically to produce profits independently, leading to the establishment of vast sugar plantations. To run the plantations, the Portuguese imported African slaves starting in the mid-fifteenth century, beginning the infamous practice that would shape the socio-political and demographic makeup of the world in a few centuries.

The main objective of finding a reliable maritime trade route through India was accomplished by the end of the century when Vasco da Gama's expedition successfully made its way around the Cape of Good Hope, through the Indian Ocean, into India, and back in 1499. This came as a relief to Portugal for interesting reasons. The obvious one was the fact that the kingdom's main rival—the Kingdom of Castille—was interested in catching up with Portugal's overseas expansion.

Castille had successfully disputed the ownership of the Canary Islands and had imposed its rule upon them early in the fifteenth century. Moreover, in 1492, Queen Isabella I of Castille agreed to fund the expedition of a certain Genoese navigator—Christopher Columbus—who believed he could find a maritime route to India by sailing west instead of south along the African coast. Underestimating the true scale of the circular Earth and unaware of another huge landmass west of Europe beyond the Atlantic, Columbus infamously made his way to the Americas instead of India.

Though offering considerably less than the wealthy lands of China or India, the Caribbean islands that Columbus explored were nevertheless claimed by the Spanish explorers. They provided a valuable outpost from which to organize further voyages onto the American continent, which promised far more riches. When the word of Columbus' first voyage spread throughout Europe after his return in 1493, the Portuguese were quick to expand their efforts, resulting in Vasco da Gama's voyage.

In 1494, Portugal and the Crown of Castille reached an agreement that shaped the future of colonial expansion. It was the adjustment of a papal bull that had granted the Crown of Castille the right to claim the lands west of an arbitrary line drawn 100 leagues west of the Azores. This was partially due to an incorrect interpretation of Columbus' first voyage, which he claimed had reached the China Sea instead of the Antilles in the Caribbean. João II of Portugal renegotiated this papal ruling with Queen Isabelle and King Ferdinand, believing it had unjustly disfavored Portugal. Under the Treaty of Tordesillas, the line was moved a bit more to the west—370 leagues west of the Cape Verde Islands. The lands that would be discovered west of the line could be claimed by Castille, whereas everything east of the line was for Portugal.

The Treaty of Tordesillas itself produced a very arbitrary demarcation, and there was no clear way of knowing which lands would belong to the Portuguese and which to the Spanish. No one was then aware of the size of the Americas, or the fact that India could be reached if one continued west from the point where Columbus had landed. Still, the unknown world promised a lot to the future colonizers.

Soon after Vasco da Gama's return in 1499, another Portuguese expedition, headed by Pedro Álvares Cabral, set sail from Lisbon. Consisting of a fleet of thirteen ships, the expedition—one of the largest of its day—had the goal of reaching the East Indies and setting up Portuguese trading activities there. Instead of sailing south along the African coast, however, the expedition took a westward route after reaching the Cape Verde Islands. About a month later, in late April of 1500, it sighted land and made landfall at Porto Seguro on the eastern coast of Brazil. The Portuguese had made their way to the New World.

Encountering the Natives

The Portuguese arrived in the New World about eight years after the Spanish. And though the two colonial enterprises would eventually take very different shapes, the colonists' initial experiences were largely the same. Besides the fact that the Europeans had no idea what lay in front of them, geographically speaking, another puzzling reality of the exploration and colonization of the New World was encountering the Amerindian population.

The Indigenous population of the Americas was very diverse, even if it could be separated into linguistic or cultural groups—something the Europeans resorted to soon after their arrival. There were two major groups in Brazil when the Portuguese arrived in 1500. The first group was the Tupi-Guarani peoples, who inhabited almost all the Brazilian coast and were the first to come in contact with the Portuguese. The Tupi mostly dwelled in the north, while the Guarani lived in the south. The underlying characteristic and reason behind these peoples' grouping together was their shared language.

The other major group in Brazil identified by the colonizers was the Tapuia—the name used as an umbrella term for all the non-Tupi-Guarani peoples of Brazil. Different tribes in these groups included the Almoré, the Tremembé, and the Goitacá, and they occupied a considerably smaller area than the Tupi-Guarani peoples.

We know little about the Indigenous population of Brazil before the arrival of Europeans. Our knowledge of their origins and ethno-cultural characteristics consists almost entirely of archeological and DNA evidence based on very recent examinations of the territories they inhabited.

The Portuguese produced very biased records against the Natives ever since their first encounters, a problem that generally plagues the narratives of early colonizers. In the writings that have survived from the early stages of colonization, we often see conflicting accounts of Native tribes, mostly based on their relations with the colonizers. Tribes that were friendlier toward the Portuguese and facilitated trade are often referred to positively in contemporary records.

On the other hand, people groups that put up more resistance against the colonizers or those who exhibited cultural characteristics denounced by the Christian way of thought were naturally viewed more negatively. All in all, the early Portuguese interactions with these different peoples produced further prejudices—some lasting for decades. For example, the Aimoré, notorious for their cannibalism (which was practiced by some groups within the Tapuia) and ferocious warfare and military skill were among the most hated Native groups. This prejudice most clearly manifested in 1570 when the ban on enslaving the Natives excluded the Aimoré.

For certain Indigenous communities, the Portuguese, with their huge ships, powerful weapons, white skin, and Christian practices, were seen as beings capable of possessing special, shamanic powers. Over time, however, as the true intentions of the Portuguese showed themselves, the Natives were forced to adapt to the new circumstances they found themselves in.

The technological superiority of the Portuguese allowed for easy military and political dominance of the Native populations. An effective strategy for the Portuguese was to forge alliances with certain tribes and use them to fight against others, contributing to the development of inter-group fighting and rivalries that eventually undermined the collective Indigenous effort to resist.

Compared to the Portuguese way of life, the social organization of the Natives was more primitive in nearly all aspects. The Indigenous populations lived in small communities and mostly pursued hunter-gatherer activities. They practiced limited, mostly subsistence agriculture and would often migrate from their dwellings once they believed the land could no longer yield crops. Interestingly, the main goods for trade were luxury items such as valuable stones or rare feathers, instead of foodstuffs. These limited trading relations ultimately determined the nature of inter-tribe relations.

The culture of Indigenous Brazilians was rather violent. Cannibalism and sacrifices were prominent practices, reserved exclusively for men, who had greater societal roles than women because they were warriors. However, archeological evidence of the pre-Columbian society of the Marajoara (Marajó) culture, centered on Marajó Island at the mouth of the Amazon River, suggests they bestowed more importance on women. They are often depicted on Marajó pottery, for example.

We will explore the relationship that developed between the colonizers and the Indigenous Amerindians of Brazil in more depth in later chapters. What we will mention here is the obvious and perhaps most horrific legacy of colonization—the decimation of the Indigenous population by diseases brought by the Europeans.

It is difficult to determine the number of Natives that lived in Brazil before the arrival of the Portuguese, with estimates ranging from a few to twelve million Indigenous people. What we can more accurately estimate is that the Indigenous population experienced a complete demographic collapse after encountering diseases for which they had developed no immunity. Smallpox spread rapidly in Indigenous societies, decimating the populations and forcing thousands to migrate inland, which did not stop the severity of the disease's effects. Only about a tenth of the Indigenous Brazilian population was lucky enough to survive after about a century of Portuguese colonization, and the number kept steadily decreasing. The demographic catastrophe brought by Portuguese colonists, coupled with their often ruthless military conquest of Native societies, accelerated the demise of Indigenous communities.

Colonizing Brazil

The first few decades after the arrival of the Portuguese in Brazil were dynamic but not as extensive as Spanish colonial activities at the time, which were centered on exploring Central America. Differently from the Spanish, who dared to venture deep inland from their bases on the Caribbean islands, the Portuguese chose to stick to the coast. They were quick to realize that the land they had reached was vastly different from India. And, since the maritime route to India around Africa had just been discovered, the Portuguese Crown was focused on establishing reliable options to India instead of to an unknown Brazil.

The Portuguese slowly explored the Brazilian coastline while engaging in trade with the Natives, who mainly harvested brazilwood for the colonists in exchange for items that were considered simple and very cheap for the Europeans, like clothing. (The land's name came from the indigenous brazilwood tree, which was not only good for making furniture items but could also be used to produce red dye, making the commodity very important.) Since the Natives already had experience communally harvesting brazilwood in several of their tribes, this relationship was profitable for both sides. This kind of activity continued for about the next three decades.

The Portuguese Crown only began to seriously invest in Brazil's colonization in the 1530s. By that time, Fernando Magellan, a Portuguese sailing under the Spanish flag, had discovered the westward maritime route to India from Europe, which passed through a narrow strait at the southern tip of South America and through the Pacific Ocean. His voyage demonstrated that it would not be a profitable endeavor to develop and pursue this route as a viable alternative to the African route discovered by Vasco da Gama.

This factor, combined with a new external threat, almost convinced the Portuguese Crown to seriously consider extensive colonization of Brazil. The threat came from the French, who had decided to try their luck in colonial endeavors. They had themselves reached the coast of Brazil, which could not be effectively defended by the Portuguese because of its size. In addition, the French did not exactly recognize the Treaty of Tordesillas, believing that it had unjustly and arbitrarily divided the world for the benefit of just two kingdoms, leaving the others out.

Ultimately, when they began to also trade for brazilwood and set up small settlements along the coast in both southern and northern Brazil, Dom João III of Portugal was forced to act. In 1530, recognizing the need for a permanent presence that would defend Portugal's trade interests, he sent an expedition to Brazil, headed by Martim Afonso de Sousa, which was tasked with defending the coastline.

Furthermore, the king decided to implement a more effective administrative system to better control the Portuguese possessions along the coast, dividing it into fifteen units, each ruled by a donatary captain (*donatários*). The captains, who came from diverse social backgrounds, were granted extensive rights over their administrative portions. They effectively ruled the land in the name of the king but did not own it. They collected fees and taxes, were obliged to explore and map their domains and form militias to defend their territories, and could divide the lands among the colonists if they saw it fit.

Yet, the captaincy system provided only a temporary solution to the colonists' problems. Most of the units were not economically successful, for example. The only captaincies that survived and emerged as later centers of Portuguese colonization were Pernambuco in the east and São Vicente in the southeast. Others failed for different reasons, such as the captains' ambitions to overextend and come into conflict with the Natives. The system nevertheless survived in several modified forms until the eighteenth century, with the roles and rights of the captains constantly changing. Significant administrative changes were implemented when Dom João III decided to set up a colonial government in Brazil with a designated governor.

Portuguese map (1574) by Luís Teixeira, showing the location of the hereditary captaincies of Brazil.[2]

This decision was partially influenced by the ongoing success of Spanish colonists in other parts of the Americas. The Spanish had established more effective ways to govern their colonial possessions and had rapidly expanded into Mexico, Central America, and the northwestern part of Southern America. The king, believing that a more centralized form of rule was needed, thus sent Tomé de Sousa to be the first royally appointed governor of Brazil in 1549 with an expedition of about a thousand men. The first governor also brought royal charters that identified the extent of his rights and proceeded to create different administrative positions concerned with judicial matters, the collection of taxes, and the patrol of the coast. There were also Christian missionaries who accompanied de Sousa, including a group of Jesuit priests whose aim it was to strictly monitor the Christian practices of the colonizers.

The new governor and his crew began to set up several large estates, mostly sugar plantations. Sugar would quickly emerge as the main commodity of Brazil aside from brazilwood. Overall, the Crown's hold on the colony became firmer, slowly resulting in economic gains and the development of a system that would last for centuries.

Chapter Two – Portuguese Brazil

Colonial Society

By the mid-sixteenth century, the Portuguese colonial enterprise in Brazil was slowly expanding. Since the Portuguese had committed to staying in their colony long-term, certain social structures began to form—structures that would define Brazil's society for centuries to come. A major aspect of the new society was the system of forced labor that was promptly put in place and grew throughout the years as the economic activity of Portuguese Brazil expanded. The Portuguese not only forced many Natives into slavery but also began to increasingly import enslaved men and women from Africa. This practice eventually became a hugely profitable endeavor in its own right while also among the worst legacies of the age of colonization.

For the colonizers, the decision to transport African slaves to Brazil was very logical. This partially stemmed from the cultural distinctions of Native Brazilian societies. As we mentioned earlier, they were not used to intensive labor and only worked as much as needed to provide for their needs.

This is not to say that the colonists did not enslave the Indigenous population. However, the Natives could also resist strongly, something that further dissuaded the colonists. Many Natives would flee the plantations they were enslaved at, going inland to the Brazilian jungles, which were still unexplored by the Portuguese. Because the Natives were more familiar with the territory they inhabited, they could more effectively run away from the colonists.

Another factor in the shift to African slave labor was the catastrophic collapse of the Native population after their encounter with the Europeans. The contraction of deadly viruses that resulted in the death of most of the Native population simply reduced the available quantity of Natives that could be enslaved by the Portuguese.

The efforts of Christian missionaries, especially the Jesuits, who sought to protect the Natives from slavery, also played a role. However, the Natives were never considered equal to the colonizers, often referred to as objects and non-human "things," even in the writings of religious figures. The Crown's measures, such as outlawing Native enslavement in the 1570s, further contributed, though many of these measures were just as arbitrary. For instance, Natives could still be enslaved if they unjustly attacked the colonizers or practiced cannibalism. Finally, the enslavement of the Indigenous population was fully outlawed in the middle of the eighteenth century, though they already composed a minor portion of Brazil's slave force before this decision.

In the eyes of the Portuguese, Africans were far more suited for the work the colonists required, which included labor-intensive sugar harvesting and refining. Slaves that were transported from Africa were also less prone to developing such deadly responses to European diseases as the Indigenous Amerindians. Though many of them died soon after arriving in Brazil, there were more of them to enslave.

The Portuguese had actively pursued the slave trade for about a century and knew how profitable it could be. By the first half of the seventeenth century, when sugar production reached its peak, so did the rate at which the Portuguese transported African slaves to Brazil. The numbers grew exponentially. It is estimated that before slavery was outlawed in the middle of the nineteenth century, as many as four million African slaves had been brought to Brazil—mostly young males who died within the first few years of arriving in South America.

The growth of Portuguese colonial activities in Brazil went hand in hand with the growth of the practice of slavery. Certain port cities, such as Rio de Janeiro and Salvador, the capital of Brazil until the middle of the eighteenth century, became centers of the Brazilian slave trade. Portuguese connections and possessions on the African coast allowed for large-scale slave trade, an enterprise in which Portugal was the leading European nation and would remain so for centuries.

The Africans who were enslaved came from diverse ethnic backgrounds. This was a deliberate practice as the colonists believed that transporting many Africans from the same communities would incite resistance movements among the slaves once they were transported to Brazil. This, combined with the vastness of the Brazilian territory and the African slaves' unfamiliarity with it, proved effective against any efforts of united resistance against the colonists.

Still, instances of runaway African slaves were common, and they would often organize communities, known as the *quilombos*, where they would establish their Indigenous practices. Though not always large, these communities were located in the peripheries of Portuguese control. Sometimes they would grow by allowing convicted and wanted white or Indigenous Amerindians to join.

Slaves made up the lowest social stratum of Brazilian colonial society, where divisions were primarily based on ethnicity and social background. This characteristic was present in all American colonial societies in different shapes and forms. White male colonists, especially those born in Portugal, were favored among the rest of the population, having access to full rights based on their social role.

The diffusion of Europeans, Indigenous groups, and Africans eventually resulted in different ethnic-based classes, such as the mulatto class, which ultimately made up most of the population in the biggest Brazilian cities. The cafusos, the name given to those with a mixture of Indigenous and African ancestry, occupied a lower position in the social hierarchy, though they were technically considered "free." It is important to understand that white colonists were always at a numerical disadvantage, especially in large urban centers such as Rio de Janeiro. Because most of the colonists were males (especially in the first decades of colonization), intermarriage and sexual intercourse with the Indigenous people was a common practice.

Prejudices about the "natural" or "God-given" inferiority of different ethnic groups held by the white colonists were supported by prominent institutions, such as the Catholic Church. Later, with the development of pseudoscientific beliefs that bestowed false importance on the physical characteristics of Africans or Indigenous people, many of these prejudices would be reinforced. According to their adherents, features such as the size of the skull or the "density" of the brain proved their inferiority to white people. These deterministic beliefs greatly influenced the makeup of Brazilian society and the social roles adopted by the different groups within it for centuries to come. Structural exploitation of those believed to have been "naturally inferior" produced further divisions that can still be observed in most post-colonial societies, including in Brazil.

Of course, there were also social distinctions within the different ethnic classes. The colonists aimed to shape Brazilian society according to European models and standards, copying the functions of the prominent social classes of medieval Portugal as closely as possible. This included the distinctions between members of the nobility, the clergy, and commoners. However, these distinctions were not as pronounced in Brazil.

Few nobles from Portugal abandoned their possessions and influence in Europe and entirely relocated to the colony because of the obvious risks associated with this move. Members of colonial society who were descendants of Portuguese nobility were referred to as *fidalgos* and were more respected than self-made colonists who had accrued great wealth by being the first to undertake colonial endeavors.

The differences in the medieval Portuguese *ancien regime* only became more prominent in the nineteenth century when the Portuguese royal family was forced to flee Lisbon and come to Brazil in exile. This defining moment in Brazilian history, and the social and political circumstances it gave rise to, will be covered in greater detail in later chapters.

Before then, the top positions in the social hierarchy were occupied by those who had the most economic power—wealthy landowners and merchants. The social movements during the Renaissance had already increased the standing of merchants in European societies, out of which a distinct upper-middle class began to form. Since they were instrumental in providing the means to transport goods to the motherland and keep the colony economically viable, their importance in the colonies grew even more.

The richest members of the landowning class, on the other hand, were plantation owners who produced sugar in large quantities thanks to the slave labor they employed. Most of the planters were not of noble origin. Instead, this group was comprised of those who had been the first to set up plantations in Brazil.

The planters and the merchants maintained a firm grip over the colonial society of Brazil. They were the driving forces behind its economy, and it was in their chief interests for the status quo to continue. Still, the two came into conflict with each other at times since their respective powers could not effectively be checked by government authorities.

Brazilian Economy

The basic organizing principle behind the colonial economic activities in Portuguese Brazil was mercantilism. Most, if not all, European nations at the time pursued a mercantilist policy, maintaining that each nation must accumulate as many resources as it could by limiting imports and relying on exports. This principle was true of the Portuguese, who saw their overseas territories, Brazil included, as a means of supplying the mother country with valuable resources that could be exported to foreign markets. In fact, diversifying the resources available to each nation was one of the main agendas of colonization. To pursue this goal and dominate international trade, European monarchies heavily regulated domestic economic activities—and Portugal was no exception.

In 1571, for example, the Portuguese Crown adopted a policy that would shape the economic activity in Brazil for centuries to come. Resources produced in Brazil were to be exclusively accessed by Portuguese merchants and traded to Portugal. No foreign merchants were allowed to approach Brazilian ports. Portuguese merchants, who had to pay a tax on goods imported to the Crown, were paying as little as possible for goods and then artificially inflating their prices when selling them. This approach, in the long term, was detrimental to colonial economies, which, despite producing huge quantities of resources for the mother countries, were unjustly compensated. The Crown, however, encouraged mercantilism by supporting the creation of state-funded and semi-private trading companies that specialized in trade with the colonies and extracted as much as they could.

The policy that granted exclusive rights to Portuguese merchants to access trade in Brazil, implemented in 1571, followed several decades of freedom of trade. To ensure that the merchants would follow the policy, the Crown needed to establish firm control over its possessions in Brazil and maintain a public order in which individuals were reminded that they were still subjects of the Portuguese monarchy. This had been one of the main goals behind the establishment of a governorship.

Additionally, public order and obedience to the Crown were guaranteed thanks to the role of the Catholic Church and the increasing presence of religious figures in Brazil, who were especially prominent from the middle of the sixteenth century. Catholic missionaries were eager to spread Catholicism, the state religion of Portugal, partially because they perceived Protestant Christian missionaries as their direct rivals. The Church and the state thus developed a mutually beneficial relationship surrounding their roles in Brazil, especially in the early days of colonization. The Crown defended the clergy and often granted it lands to set up monasteries in the colony. Through its constant involvement in the everyday life of the Brazilian-Portuguese subjects, the Church was a guarantor of order and had a free hand in spreading Catholicism. It also paid a portion of its earnings to the Crown.

The economic output of Brazil was diverse, with regions specializing in the production of different goods. At first, the northeastern part of the colony was the most important economically, stemming from the fact that it was the first area colonized by the Portuguese. The coastal city of Salvador, now in the modern-day state of Bahia, was the capital of the colony until 1763, stimulating growth and production around the city.

This part of the colony depended on the production and export of sugar, one of the most valuable commodities in the world in the sixteenth and seventeenth centuries. A century earlier, it had become a staple of European cuisine instead of a luxury product. The colonists soon set up a system that maximized sugar production. Aided by a very suitable climate for growing sugar, Brazil experienced an economic boom during these years. The northeastern captaincies profited the most, thanks in part to their relative proximity to European ports and rich soil that was irrigated by the Amazon River.

The Crown aided the development of the sugar economy in Brazil by, for example, exempting sugar planters from paying additional taxes on their earnings. This incentivized more and more people to plant sugar even though sugar harvesting was a tenuous, labor-intensive, and intricate process requiring great skill, perfect conditions, and adequate equipment. Because of the expensive nature of sugar production, planters usually borrowed money from all sorts of creditors, including religious institutions and independent Catholic orders that enjoyed special financial privileges. Later, planters developed a symbiotic relationship with wealthy merchants, who often financed the establishment of sugar plantations and, in turn, purchased sugar from the planters at a reduced price.

By the late sixteenth century, efforts to encourage sugar production also had the indirect effect of increasing the number of African slave laborers who worked on the plantations. Processing sugar required intensive labor, which, in turn, took a physical toll on those who worked in the fields. Since the Portuguese colonists viewed African slaves as essentially disposable resources, they increasingly relied on them to harvest sugar. This resulted in the deaths of tens of thousands of slaves, many of whom, as we mentioned earlier, died from overworking or horrific living conditions.

Since the demand for African slaves increased during this period, more and more slaves were transported from Portugal's African holdings to Brazil, and their prices began to rise, as well. Many planters, who had greatly increased their wealth and influence by the middle of the seventeenth century, could afford more and more slaves, further increasing their profits.

Brazil essentially held a monopoly in sugar production and almost single-handedly supplied European markets for decades until other colonies increasingly began to harvest sugar themselves. The Caribbean colonies of France and England emerged as the main competitors for Brazil.

Although Brazil's economic output increasingly diversified in the later decades of the seventeenth century as a response to the new rivals, sugar nevertheless remained a central product. Sugar made up about half of all Brazilian exports in the eighteenth century, though its profitability had greatly decreased from its heyday a century and a half earlier. Later, international factors like the slave rebellion in the French colony of Saint Domingue (Haiti)— the largest sugar producer in the world at the time— revived the profitability of Brazilian sugar. The rebellion, which turned into a full-on revolution in Haiti, greatly disrupted sugar production on the island and incentivized merchants to visit neighboring colonial markets to buy sugar.

Cotton, tobacco, brazilwood, coffee, and manioc were also among the goods produced in Brazil. Domestically, many landowners also began to raise cattle, which became a vital part of the Brazilian agricultural market. Crucially, at the end of the seventeenth century, gold was discovered in the southern parts of Brazil, inciting a gold rush. Gold, for obvious reasons, quickly became the main Brazilian export alongside sugar and greatly contributed to the development of southern Brazil, which had previously been considered a periphery. It also motivated the colonists to move deeper inland and explore the mysterious hinterlands of Brazil, resulting in the founding of new settlements. The Brazilian gold rush ultimately shaped the socio-economic dynamics of the colony in the eighteenth century, which we will explore in greater detail later.

Crisis in Brazil

Throughout the sixteenth century, Brazil thus began to develop into an important overseas possession of Portugal. Though it could not boast the abundance of precious metals that were present in Spain's American colonies, it nevertheless gradually expanded its economic output, attracting notice from the motherland. More and more colonists began to emigrate to Portuguese Brazil. The coastline was studied very well, and several expeditions even journeyed into the interior with hopes of finding more wealth.

It was between the sixteenth and the seventeenth centuries that Portuguese possessions in Brazil began to face their first significant threat. This stemmed from the complex international political climate that emerged in the late 1500s as the European kingdoms engaged in continent-wide conflicts that also affected their overseas territories.

In 1578, the Portuguese monarchy experienced a succession crisis after the death of King Sebastian I, who left no heirs. His great-uncle Henry, a cardinal of the Catholic Church, ruled the kingdom for the next two years. But after he died in 1580, the Crown was left without an heir once again. Different contenders emerged for the Portuguese throne, but the nobility chose Spain's King Philip II as the new king. This resulted in the establishment of the Iberian Union—about sixty years during which the Spanish branch of the House of Habsburg ruled Spain (itself a union of the crowns of Castille and Aragon) and Portugal. The Habsburg rulers had also inherited possessions in Italy and the Netherlands, making them the most powerful dynasty in Europe at the time.

The Iberian Union meant that the Spanish and the Portuguese could temporarily disregard the line of the Tordesillas Treaty, the century-old agreement that was still respected by the two. Interested parties from both kingdoms, most importantly wealthy merchants and colonists in the Americas, hoped to gain easier access to previously unexplored markets and profit from the new political situation.

During this period, several large-scale expeditions into the heart of South America were first organized by the Portuguese, who crossed the arbitrary border set by the Treaty of Tordesillas and ventured into the Amazon. Though no permanent large settlements were established in what became the central-westernmost part of modern-day Brazil, the state of Mato Grosso, these expeditions provided valuable leverage for the Portuguese to claim the unexplored South American lands.

On the other hand, being in a personal union with the Spanish Crown meant that the Portuguese were also drawn into the conflicts fought by the Spanish Habsburgs. At the time, the Spanish Crown was facing a rebellion from its subjects in the Netherlands—a conflict that had begun in the 1560s and would eventually last until the middle of the seventeenth century. Covering intricate details of the Dutch Revolt against the Spanish Habsburgs is beyond the scope of this book, but what we do need to establish is that the Dutch, having colonial designs, began to attack Portuguese possessions in Africa, Asia, and South America. They raided Salvador in 1604 and were a menacing threat to Portuguese ships in the Atlantic for the next few years.

Despite a twelve-year truce between the Spanish and the Dutch from 1609 to 1621 during which the Portuguese colony enjoyed a brief period of peace, the Dutch began to increasingly eye Portuguese territories in South America. Attracted by the lucrative sugar industry, the Dutch created the Dutch West India Company to gain control of the weakly defended colonies in South America and emerge as the new colonial superpower. In Asia, the Dutch East Indies Company pursued similar goals against Portugal's Asian colonies.

Three years after the truce was broken, in 1624, the Dutch attacked Salvador again and occupied it without much resistance. The attack came as another shock to the Portuguese colonists in Brazil, who fled Salvador and utilized guerilla tactics for the next few months to keep the Dutch forces from expanding their control beyond the city. It was only in May of 1625, after the arrival of a force of more than 10,000 soldiers from Europe, that the Dutch surrendered Salvador and gave control of the city back to the Portuguese.

In 1630, the Dutch returned with a new force, now attacking northeastern Brazil and taking the coastal cities of Recife and Olinda. This time, the Portuguese were unable to drive the Dutch back so quickly due to the help they received from local Portuguese colonists.

The Dutch West India Company established its headquarters in Recife and slowly began to conquer the coastal territories further to the north. What emerged was Dutch Brazil, or, as the Dutch themselves referred to the colony, New Holland. Portuguese guerilla fighters nevertheless made it difficult for the Dutch to profit from sugar production for the next few years.

The struggle for control of northeastern Brazil would continue until 1654. By then, Portugal was no longer in a personal union with the Spanish Crown, and the Dutch had finally gained their independence from the Habsburgs after eighty years of fighting. However, the Portuguese still intended to take back what they had lost to the Dutch in the 1630s.

Thanks to resistance efforts from local leaders such as João Fernandes Vieira and André Vidal de Negreiros, Portuguese colonists in Brazil began to achieve small victories over the Dutch positions. The center of the insurrection against the Dutch was the rural area of Pernambuco, and the victories eventually reduced Dutch holdings to Recife. The locals emerged victorious in the two decisive battles of Guararapes in 1648 and 1649, further weakening the position of the Dutch in Brazil.

In early 1652, due to the growing tensions between the Netherlands and England over their possessions in North America, the two states went to war, taking a tremendous toll on the Dutch war effort in Brazil. At this pivotal moment, King João VI of Portugal finally decided to send a large naval squadron to expel the Dutch from Recife once and for all. They surrendered to the Portuguese forces in January of 1654.

Consolidation and Expansion

The war against the Dutch highlighted obvious problems that had existed in the colonial system. The inability to defend key coastal cities from Dutch assaults made it clear that Portugal had long ignored the defense of its valuable colony. Though the Crown ultimately reacted to the invasion and occupation of Brazil by the Dutch forces, victory was ultimately thanks to the efforts of locals. Moreover, the Dutch had also briefly occupied the Portuguese possessions in Africa, in modern-day Angola. This had partially disrupted the influx of African slaves to Brazil and had further hindered stabilization after the war. All in all, Portugal's economy took a great hit during the middle of the seventeenth century, and the country barely retained control of Brazil, where the colonizers were eager to resume imperial exploitation for material gains.

Still, increasing efforts had been made since the late sixteenth century to further explore the Brazilian interior. The obvious route was up the Amazon River in the northern part of the country. No one knew the extent of the rainforests, let alone the path the river took before its mouth opened at the Atlantic Ocean. Exploring this part of the continent promised to be a worthy endeavor because it could potentially link the Portuguese possessions with the Spanish colonies in the northern and western parts of South America. The coastal town of Belém, founded in 1616 at the mouth of the Amazon, served this purpose and was a point of resistance against the French, who occupied lands further north (territories that eventually became French Guiana).

In 1637, Portuguese explorer Pedro Teixeira became the first European to successfully journey the whole length of the Amazon River, reaching Spanish Peru and claiming the vast lands of the Amazon jungle for the Portuguese colony in the process. This part of Brazil, now organized into the states of Para and Amazonas, remained underdeveloped, however, with a large concentration of Indigenous people. It could not specialize in large-scale agricultural production, such as the cultivation of sugar or cotton, was very poor, and was still very unexplored.

The dense tropical rainforests dissuaded most explorers from trying their luck in the area, but not all feared leading expeditions deeper inland—especially those with a divine mission to spread the word of God. Yes, the effort to explore northern and central Brazil was spearheaded by Christian missionaries, especially the Jesuit groups, who began founding small villages and converted tens of thousands of indigenous Amerindians to Catholicism by the middle of the eighteenth century.

Overall, the Jesuits were against the systemic violence practiced against Indigenous people, and the colonists sometimes viewed them unfavorably for this reason. Since they had obtained support from the Indigenous people, many saw their growing influence in the region as potentially damaging to the future cohesion of the colony. Consequently, the Jesuits were temporarily expelled from the area in 1684. They eventually returned and continued missionary activities until 1752, when the Crown banned their activities in northern Brazil.

Early efforts had also been made to expand south, where the city of São Paulo had been founded in 1554 by a group of Jesuit missionaries.

Named after Paul the Apostle and located on a convenient plateau about 800 meters above sea level, São Paulo, acted as a center from which missions were launched for the first several decades of its existence. The main reason for this was, again, the larger presence of Indigenous groups. In fact, the northern and southernmost regions of Brazil were similar in many other ways as well. Both regions had a weaker economic output and a stronger influence of Jesuit missionaries. Portuguese colonists often intermarried with the Natives, giving rise to the *mameluco* class, a word used to refer to the offspring of white colonists and Natives.

São Paulo also acted as an important center for further exploration to the south and west. Expeditionary settlers were referred to as *bandeirantes*. The name comes from the Portuguese word for flag—*bandeira*—as the expeditions were headed by designated flag bearers and old Portuguese military units containing up to fifty men. The *bandeirantes* played a very important role in the expansion of colonial Brazil's borders well beyond the line of Tordesillas. Their expeditions were made up of local Paulista (residents of São Paulo) *mamelucos*, and white colonists, who were in charge. The expeditions were

A painting of Brazilian bandeirantes.[3]

supported by large numbers of Indigenous Amerindians, who followed the colonists' lead and were instrumental in navigating the unknown areas of southern Brazil.

The *bandeirantes* journeyed in all directions from São Paulo, regularly encountering previously uncontacted villages of Natives and enslaving the Indigenous population. Their expeditions sometimes took several years to complete, and many of them were organized independently from the colonial government's support. Of course, the

Portuguese bureaucrats in charge of the São Vicente captaincy and beyond generally welcomed the *bandeirantes'* efforts to explore the remote areas, especially since they further spread Portuguese control over the Native-dominated areas.

Imprisoned Amerindians from these remote villages were mostly sold as slaves in the south, mostly in Rio de Janeiro, where there was a new demand for slave labor due to the recent development of the sugar industry. Extensive *bandeirante* activities coincided with the years when the steady supply of African slaves to Brazil was disrupted due to the ongoing war with the Dutch.

Bandeirante expeditions were also vital to the history of colonial Brazil in another aspect. In the late seventeenth century, in the modern-day mountainous state of Minas Gerais, the *bandeirantes* discovered gold. As one can imagine, this greatly affected the socio-economic dynamics of colonial Brazil, prompting a gold rush that led thousands of colonists to undertake journeys into the unknown in search of the precious metal. This was especially true for many who came directly from Portugal to southern Brazil in search of new and prosperous lives. It is estimated that more than half a million Portuguese came to Brazil during the first few decades after the discovery of gold.

This discovery fueled the economy of the southern part of the colony, which had previously been overshadowed by the richer sugar-producing areas in the northeast. Now, however, the northeast slowly began to lose its economic and political importance. Sugar production had already been hit hard during the wars with the Dutch, and the rising demand for slave labor and increasing emigration to the south had their consequences. This was best manifested in 1763, when the colony's capital was transferred from Salvador to Rio de Janeiro, which quickly became the fastest-growing city in Brazil alongside São Paulo.

Another effect of the discovery of gold was that the Portuguese Crown became more interested in regulating its colony, leading to the establishment of new administrative demarcations and important civil services, such as town tribunals and courts. Gold was also heavily taxed, with at least a fifth of all mined precious metals (diamond was also discovered but in a much smaller quantity) going directly to the royal treasury. Colonist miners were also taxed based on the amount of slaves they employed. Those who were independent, meaning they had no slaves, also had to pay additional fees.

The extent to which the motherland suddenly became involved in the everyday life of colonial Brazil was remarkable. The Crown also tried to balance the interests of different regions of its colony. The inhabitants of São Paulo had initially requested special privileges regarding access to gold mines, but it was not in the interest of Lisbon to openly favor one part of the colony over another. Quotas for slaves were introduced in the south to make sure that slave supply to the northeastern sugar plantations remained stable.

Yet, such rapid and active involvement in the affairs of the newest colonial region had its consequences. Both European and *mameluco* colonists began to distrust centrally appointed authorities, who increasingly disregarded their demands in order to accrue as much profit for the Crown as possible. With the mining economy growing thanks to the increased supply of slaves, the wealthiest colonists in the southern region gained much influence and political power. Many wealthy landowners, some of them sugar planters, also diversified their incomes by becoming involved in the mining business.

The discovery of gold also contributed to the development of new sectors of the economy centered on gold, creating opportunities for directly extracting the resource. This reached its peak in the middle of the eighteenth century and slowly began to decline, with Brazilian gold mines gradually running dry by the nineteenth century.

Chapter Three – The Birth of Independent Brazil

Wrestling with the Motherland

A period of true social and political turbulence began in Brazil in the second half of the eighteenth century. At the core of this upheaval were, once again, broader international developments in Europe that forever transformed the fate of the continent and its people. The absolutist monarchic structure of European kingdoms and empires began to show its cracks as the Age of Enlightenment brought new ideas about self-governance and personal liberties. Major British and French thinkers challenged the absolutist status quo with their writings, asserting the fundamental principles of liberalism upon which the modern Western world would eventually be founded.

These liberal ideas manifested in a series of crises experienced by some of the most powerful European empires, resulting in the outbreak of the Thirteen Colonies' war of independence from Great Britain in 1776. The revolutionaries defeated the British forces, founding the United States of America, which posed a threat to the imperial designs of the Europeans. In addition, the French Revolution, which began in 1789, brought a significant paradigm shift in Europe. With the French King Louis XVI overthrown, the revolutionaries proclaimed a republic and proceeded to implement radical measures that threatened other monarchies around the continent.

Hand in hand with these political developments were socio-economic shifts. The Industrial Revolution ushered in an era of previously unseen economic development thanks to the invention of new machinery and the use of new sources of energy to perform labor. The development of local factories boosted the productivity of European industry and manufacturing, resulting in higher levels of urbanization that positively impacted economic development.

The events of the mid-to-late eighteenth century and the ideas they were based on had their foundation in the breakthroughs in science and philosophy during the Renaissance, which had also kickstarted the Age of Discovery that had made certain European powers masters of the New World. Now, however, these same ideas, further developed (and, in some cases, radicalized), posed a threat to the same colonial possessions.

In the ever-changing Western world, Portugal was a clear loser. Compared to France, and, especially, Britain—which had spearheaded the Industrial Revolution and gotten a head start in economic development—Portugal greatly lagged.

The British, who were rapidly industrializing and adopting new economic policies to ensure further growth of their domestic and overseas markets, tried to exploit the weakness of Portugal's and Spain's colonial possessions. They also began to abandon their long-standing mercantilist practices and started to practice free trade. Even after having lost their possessions in North America in the American Revolutionary War, the British were slowly emerging as the new hegemon of the world. Their relatively stable political system allowed them to dominate their rivals overseas. They were increasingly involved in the economic activities of other European colonies, which still followed the principles of exclusivity that put local merchants at a disadvantage. The British often secretly negotiated with foreign merchants to gain access to their markets, encouraging smuggling and other illegal activities that damaged the colonial incomes of Spain and Portugal.

The Portuguese, on the other hand, tried to keep up with the rapidly modernizing world, though they were reluctant to completely abandon the *ancien regime*. Although they began to take measures to rival the British with the reforms undertaken during the reign of Dom José I, they were too late. By the late eighteenth century, Brazil's gold mines were starting to run dry, and the emergence of other large sugar manufacturers caused an economic crisis in the colony. Back in Portugal, Lisbon had almost completely been destroyed by a massive earthquake in 1755, and funds were directed toward rebuilding the capital. In South America, Portuguese explorers were increasingly clashing with the Spanish over the southern territories, which put a further toll on the kingdom.

As a response, the Crown tried to further centralize its rule over the colonies and gain firmer control over its economic output. For example, as we mentioned, the Crown decided to expel the Jesuits from Brazil in 1759. The possessions of the religious order were confiscated and either completely seized or redistributed. Factories were also set up in the urban areas of Brazil to incentivize local production and not be completely reliant on raw materials as the main source of income for Brazil's economy. Portugal also encouraged efforts to further integrate the Indigenous population into colonial society, politically dominated by white colonists and mixed-race individuals. To this end, the Crown abolished Indigenous slavery in 1757, as mentioned earlier.

Yet, these measures were not enough to significantly change the socio-economic landscape in Brazil, where many began to blame their problems on their colonial overlords. Brazilians closely observed the developments in other European colonies, especially in the United States, which was an example of successful resistance against colonial powers and the assertion of the right of self-governance. Liberal ideas motivated groups to organize local conspiracy movements in different regions of Brazil. Though these movements laid the foundation for a national consciousness that later resulted in Brazilian independence, they were not widely supported in the colony. The dominant classes of colonial Brazil, including wealthy landowners and merchants, largely supported maintaining the status quo of social inequality, though they also believed that independence from Portugal could greatly increase their personal gains.

Out of the late eighteenth-century conspiracies in Brazil, the Inconfidência Mineira stands out the most. Its leaders, the *inconfidentes*, were members of the Minas Gerais elite and included several rich landowners, colonial military and government officials, lawyers, and businessmen who had ties with both the colonial regime in Brazil and Europe. Influenced by the prominent liberal ideas of the time, they recognized the declining social state of their region, plagued by economic crises and corruption. Their goal was to overthrow the colonial government and organize a constitutional republic modeled after the United States. The separatists supported the abolition of slavery in Brazil and the subsequent creation of an egalitarian, independent society.

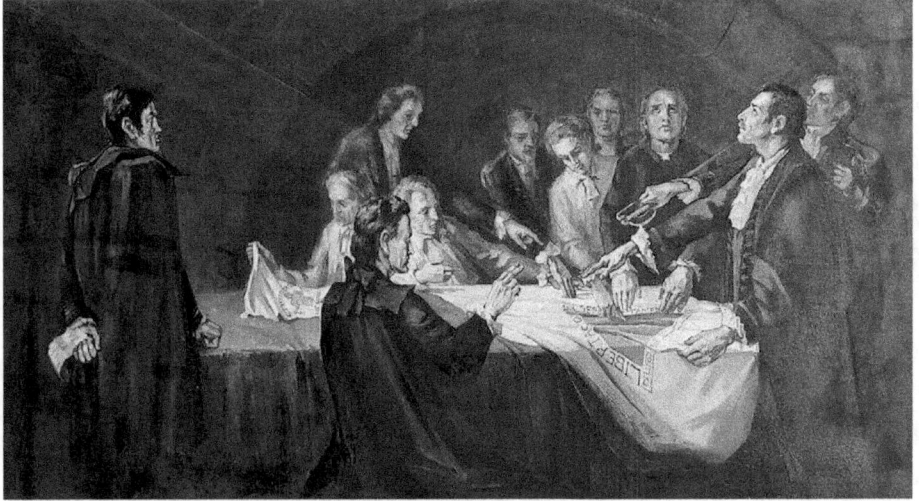

The inconfidentes by Carlos Oswald.'

Despite developing plans as early as 1788, the *inconfidentes* were never able to act, and their conspiracy was soon discovered. Imprisoned and trialed for the next couple of years, they were sentenced to death by hanging in 1792. The body of one of their members, a low-ranking military officer named Joaquim José da Silva Xavier—better known by his nickname *Tiradentes*, or "Tooth Puller"—was cut to pieces after the execution, and his head was put on public display at the town square of Ouro Preto. Though the Inconfidência Mineira did not materialize into any gains for the local Brazilians against the Portuguese colonizers, the symbolic importance of the movement remained in the colonists' consciousness. Eventually, Tiradentes, who had claimed responsibility for leading the insurrection despite playing a relatively small part in it, became a national hero of independent Brazil. As a martyr who died for freedom, he still lives on in the memory of Brazilians.

Monarchy in Brazil

The beginning of the nineteenth century brought another unique development, influenced by the circumstances in Europe, that greatly affected the future of Brazil. Having emerged as the emperor of France after the chaos of the French Revolution, Napoleon Bonaparte waged a war against most of Europe in the first decade of the 1800s. The success of the French in the early stages of the Napoleonic Wars had resulted in their total domination of Western Europe and an economic embargo on Great Britain—Napoleon's main adversary and the only power he could not decisively defeat. The Continental System, set up in 1806, prohibited any of France's European client states from trading with the British. The system was enforced by the French, though some countries, such as Russia, still secretly practiced trade with Great Britain.

Another exception to the blockade was Portugal, which had so far remained neutral in the wars against France and had been defensively allied with the British. Believing that the trade between the British and the Portuguese endangered his goals in Europe, the French general decided to invade Portugal through his client state of Spain in November 1807.

Portugal was not prepared for an all-out war against the French, and not only because of the superiority of the veteran French forces. The Crown was also in a political crisis at the time. The ruling Queen Maria I, who had experienced the deaths of her husband, Dom Peter III, and her son and heir to the throne, Prince Joseph, had developed problems with her mental state and could not effectively govern the kingdom. In her stead, rulership had been assumed by her younger son, Prince João, who would become Dom João VI of Portugal in 1816 after his mother's death.

João VI of Portugal.[5]

Acting as regent in the most critical period of the throne, the young prince knew he could not put up a fight against Napoleon's French war machine. Instead, he made the very interesting decision to flee Portugal to Brazil.

Upon hearing of the French invasion, João, escorted by the British armada, decided to transfer the royal court to Rio de Janeiro, leaving the kingdom in Europe free for Napoleon's taking. In late November of 1807, the young prince, accompanied by some 15,000 people, including state bureaucrats and officials, members of the royal family, judges, nobility, important religious figures, and army and naval officers, set sail for South America.

In a move that shocked the Portuguese population, the prince took everything he deemed valuable for the functioning of the Crown to deny the French control over the Portuguese government apparatuses. This included the royal treasury, printing presses, and royal archives. People were right in thinking that their suzerain had abandoned them, cowardly fleeing a confrontation with Napoleon's forces. João and his court had tried to tell his subjects to remain calm and not resist the invaders, saying that the royal family would one day return, though this did little to dissuade the panic.

The journey to Brazil was long and tenuous. Overcrowding in the ships was a major problem, causing a shortage of supplies and poor sanitary conditions that resulted in the outbreak of several diseases and many deaths. The ships also greatly suffered from storms in the Atlantic that separated parts of the navy and created organizational problems. Finally, João and most of the ships arrived in Salvador, rather than Rio, where the prince's mother and other members of the royal family were transported. The reason behind the change of destination is unclear, though it was probably done to assert the political significance of the old capital. His court only briefly stayed in Salvador, however, continuing the journey to Rio in about a month and beginning a new era in the history of Brazil.

The transfer of the monarchy to Brazil was a unique instance in the history of European colonization and was followed by significant social and political developments in Rio and elsewhere. Many problems needed to be addressed in Brazil, some of them brought by the thousands of new immigrants and others rooted in the historical development of the colony. One of the first measures of Prince João's administration was to open the Brazilian ports to foreign ships—a decree that aimed to normalize trade relations with Britain.

Witnessing the ongoing situation in Brazil prompted the prince's administration to adopt other significant changes directed at boosting

Brazil's economy. The Crown began to support the Brazilian economy by directly investing in the creation of factories to boost local manufacturing and providing subsidies for different industries. Many tariffs, part of the old mercantilist system, were abolished to encourage domestic and international trade.

Though these changes brought positive improvements to Brazil, the British benefitted the most, economically speaking. João's decrees essentially legalized trade with the British merchants, who had practiced contraband trade in Brazilian ports for many decades. The fate of Portugal as an independent kingdom in Europe was largely dependent on Great Britain and its war against the French, a reality that gave the British a lot of political influence. A part of the British Royal Navy also defended Brazil's coast in case of a foreign invasion, as the Portuguese Crown had no resources to muster up a competent navy. The British used this influence to strike even more profitable agreements with the Portuguese in Brazil, guaranteeing advantages for British products that flowed into Brazil's ports.

On the other hand, it soon became clear to many Brazilians that the royal court's residence in Brazil did not exactly mean prosperity. The Crown was still acting in its own interests and largely disregarding the demands of the local population. Because effective control over the European territories had been lost, Brazilians were now overtaxed. And, as mentioned earlier, freedom from trade restrictions did not alleviate the new tax burden. Additionally, some of the measures taken by Prince João resulted in further instability. He organized several military expeditions to the south with the hopes of gaining control over Banda Oriental on the River Plate, where the Portuguese had contested Spanish claims for over a century.

This discontent with the new regime was best manifested in the Pernambuco rebellion of 1817, during which the entire northeastern province revolted against the newly crowned Dom João VI. The rebels blamed the king for favoring not only the Portuguese members of his kingdom over the locals but also the southern Brazilians over the northerners. A strong regional identity had been a staple of Pernambuco, and it is no surprise that the movement against the Crown in 1817 was very heterogeneous, with most sectors of Pernambuco's society participating in the revolt. Beginning from the city of Recife, the revolt eventually spread to other parts of Brazil, making it the first significant threat to Dom João's safety since his arrival in Brazil.

However, the diverse composition of the rebellion also meant that the different groups had joined the movement to pursue their own ends, destabilizing the whole effort. The royal forces were thus subdued the rebellion in May and executed its leaders in Recife.

From a Colony to an Empire

By then, the Napoleonic Wars had ended with the defeat of the French, and the antebellum status quo was restored in Europe. The victors pushed for the strengthening of conservative monarchies on the continent. This meant that Dom João and his court could return to Portugal and rule the colony from there. However, João decided to stay in Brazil, choosing to inaugurate the former colony into a united kingdom with its former colonial motherland. What resulted was the Kingdom of Portugal, Brazil and the Algarves—a union in which the overseas territories of Portugal were at least nominally equal in status.

The new kingdom was short-lived, however. Dom João's decision to stay in Brazil with his court had seemed strange to the Portuguese in Europe, and so did the proclamation of a new union with Brazil and the Algarves. In 1820, a military uprising in the city of Porto resulted in the outbreak of a liberal revolution in Portugal, with the revolutionaries setting up a junta government and ruling in the name of the king. The aim of the revolution, inspired by the liberal ideas of the Enlightenment, was to address the ongoing ambiguity in Portugal with the absence of the king and other government entities.

Though the revolutionaries were against the institution of absolute monarchy, the nature of the revolution was not fully "liberal," as they supported Portugal's control over its overseas territories. This was characteristic of other liberal movements around the same time. During the Haitian Revolution a few decades earlier, for example, many French liberals had advocated for the French army to quell the rebellion and retake control over Haiti, which provided mainland France with valuable resources and was a driving force behind its economy. The Portuguese revolutionaries mostly thought along the same lines in 1820.

The revolutionaries also decided to call for the convention and reformation of the Cortes. The Cortes was an old Portuguese assembly where representatives of the nobility, clergy, and the bourgeoisie from Portugal's different provinces sometimes convened at the demand of the king to assist him in crucial matters. It was similar to the Estates-General in France, an institution where disputes between the different social groups had sparked the French Revolution in 1789. The main demand of the revolutionaries was for the king to return to Portugal and for the Cortes to become the overarching institution, with representatives from all the territories under Portugal's control. The goal was to write a constitution and reform the country according to liberal beliefs, though not all was yet set in place.

Dom João, considering his plan of action after hearing the news from Europe, was in the meantime confronted with a local rebellion in the armed forces that fueled widespread discontent in the urban areas of Brazil. Finally, though the king feared that returning to Lisbon would end his rule, he was forced to acquiesce to the demands of the rebels, setting sail for Portugal in April 1821 with the royal court accompanying him. He installed his son, Prince Pedro, as the regent of Brazil to rule in his stead.

Meanwhile, the Cortes convened in Portugal to discuss the fate of the kingdom and its overseas territories. During their assemblies over the year, Portuguese members of the Cortes repeatedly denounced any idea of Brazilian self-governance and patronized the Brazilians, whom they saw as subordinates to Portuguese rule. In an interesting turn of events, the representatives ruled in favor of integrating the Brazilian provinces directly under the jurisdiction of Portugal, which essentially degraded Brazil's status back to an overseas colony of Portugal. The representatives also recalled many of the high-ranking Portuguese officers who had remained in Brazil back to Lisbon and demanded the same from Prince Pedro as well.

The pressure mounted on the young prince, as a very prominent liberal Brazilian faction advocated for a break with Portugal. This was also supported by several Portuguese officials residing in Brazil at the time, who organized a petition to convince the prince to disobey the Cortes' orders. Among the main Brazilian liberals was José Bonifácio de Andrada, who would play an important role in the events of the following few years.

Finally, on January 9, 1822, Prince Pedro made his decision to stay in Brazil and defy the demands of the Portuguese revolutionaries. The event became known as the *Dia do Fico*, or "I Shall Stay Day" and marked a significant turning point in Brazilian history. Word soon spread of his pivotal decision. Virtually all of Brazil supported the young prince, though some tried to organize a coup to end Pedro's designs to make Brazil an autonomous state. A quick rebellion was organized by a contingent of Portuguese troops that remained in Brazil, led by officer Jorge Avillez. The rebels quickly found themselves outnumbered. Dom Pedro, instead of punishing the soldiers, offered them the opportunity to set sail for Portugal. Some who swore fealty to the new ruler of Brazil decided to stay and became part of the new army being organized, with José Bonifácio de Andrada as its leader.

Things moved quickly during the next few months. As was usually the case among liberal revolutionaries of the time, different factions emerged that envisioned rather different futures for Brazil before Pedro could consolidate his position and officially declare independence. The conservative wing of Brazilians, including Bonifácio, believed that Brazil should be organized into a constitutional monarchy with an elected government but limited voting rights to certain groups in Brazilian society. More radical liberals preferred universal suffrage, and some even hoped to abolish the monarchy or limit the monarch's powers—though most recognized that the latter scenario was not as likely.

The Portuguese Cortes, upon hearing about the developments that had unfolded in Brazil, sent back word rejecting the actions of the prince and urging him to come back to Lisbon once again. When the news of the Cortes' demands reached Pedro, who was near the Ipiranga River, traveling to São Paulo, he delivered these famous words to his companions: "*Independência ou Morte!*" ("Independence or Death!"). On December 1, 1822, he would be proclaimed the first Emperor of Brazil as Dom Pedro I.

The First Reign

From late 1822 onward, things moved very quickly in the newly independent Empire of Brazil. Dom Pedro I's decision to proclaim independence from Portugal was naturally met with a lot of resistance. Lisbon tried to prepare an adequate response for what it considered treason from the royal prince. Because of stark regional differences and identities, there was no consensus among the different provinces of Brazil. Some, especially in the north, declared their support for Portugal. Nevertheless, the former colonial power could do little to force Brazilians back into subordination. The Portuguese Cortes was in no position to send a large force to South America and could only rely on the pockets of resistance that remained in parts of Brazil to gain control of the colony.

Dom Pedro quickly built a local Brazilian army, and many of his supporters even began organizing local militias to put up a fight against those who resisted. Many slaves were also freed in exchange for their conscription in the army, resulting in the impressive growth of the Brazilian forces by early 1823. What followed was a brief war of independence during which the remaining Portuguese troops in Brazil separately fought against the Brazilian forces loyal to Dom Pedro.

Initially, the Portuguese forces took control of some of the major Brazilian cities, like Salvador and Recife. However, they were quickly forced to surrender, outnumbered by the Brazilians. The Brazilians dominated the Portuguese on the seas, with many Portuguese switching sides and declaring their allegiance to Pedro and his cause. Most Portuguese forces were defeated or fled by sea by late 1823, and the war was largely over.

What followed was months of stalling from the Portuguese government. Not wanting to give up its hopes of maintaining control over Brazil, it tried to negotiate with local interest groups and international actors. But, by 1824, Dom Pedro had consolidated his position in the newly independent Brazil. Additionally, some foreign powers, most importantly the United States, recognized Brazilian independence, reducing the bargaining chips available for Lisbon. Britain also supported an independent Brazil, seeing it as a viable solution for the protection of its trade interests in South America. Britain did not formally recognize Brazil's independence because they demanded that Brazil end its involvement in the slave trade. However, this was not an immediate option as the country's economy was largely dependent on slave labor.

With the coup of the summer of 1823, Dom João VI regained absolute power in Portugal, further complicating the political situation. Finally, Lisbon agreed to recognize the independence of Brazil after extensive negotiations and mediation from Britain. In August 1825, Brazil agreed to pay a hefty sum of two million British pounds to Portugal as reparations for the economic damages inflicted on Lisbon with the loss of the colony in exchange for recognition. This extremely large amount of capital was simply not available for Dom Pedro at the time, so the emperor's administration was forced to borrow the sum from the British banks. Despite the unfavorable terms, the Brazilian emperor knew that he had to gain recognition from Portugal if he wanted other European nations to formally recognize an independent

Brazil and normalize relations.

Domestically, the main political concern for the newly independent Brazil was the question of how it would organize the new government. In May 1823, members of the new constituent assembly first convened to work on the country's constitution and define judicial, legislative, and executive powers and competencies. Extensive negotiations and political maneuvering lasted for about a year until the first constitution was adopted in March 1824.

For its time, it was quite a liberal document and also quite unique. Compared to other Latin American countries that had recently become independent from Spain, Brazil was the only one with a monarchical system. This meant that, initially, there were concerns about the status and role of the emperor and the extent of his powers concerning the parliamentary system the liberal reformers wished to introduce. There were also questions regarding the status of the nobility and other institutions from the *ancien regime*, like the role of the Catholic Church.

Dom Pedro I of Brazil.[6]

The constitution that was eventually adopted and ratified would be kept in place with few modifications until the end of the Brazilian Empire. It was influenced by other similar documents of the time. The 1824 Constitution guaranteed the fundamental individual freedoms of thought and assembly, the equality of all citizens before the law, and religious freedoms (though Roman Catholicism was made the official religion, and other religions could only be practiced privately).

Politically, it instituted a constitutional monarchy where the legislative branch— made up of the Chamber of Deputies and the Senate—was to be elected through indirect and restricted voting. Voting rights were not extended to all of Brazil's population, and certain economic requirements must be met to run for office and be eligible to vote. Only men with an income of at least 100 milreis could vote, but they did not directly choose their candidates. On the other hand, only Catholic males with an annual income of at least 400 milreis could run as a deputy in the lower chamber. Three candidates would be chosen as representatives from each province in the Senate, with the emperor having a final say in who would become a senator—an office that was for life.

The voters voted for an electoral college, which then elected the deputies. Administratively, the province system was mostly kept intact, but the emperor could elect the individual presidents who governed each province. A special Council of State was also introduced, comprised of counselors over forty years old with over 800 milreis of income who served for life and were appointed by the emperor. The role of the Council was to provide advice to the emperor in critical times, though the Council itself had no executive or legislative powers. In addition to the powers mentioned above, the emperor could dissolve the Chamber of Deputies and had a final say on the laws adopted by the parliament, with a right to veto any decision of either body.

Overall, the social and political system of the Empire of Brazil was very distinct from that of other former colonies that had gained independence around the same time, and even from some of the systems put in place in Europe. It was a rather conservative constitutional monarchy, with voting restricted to a clearly defined portion of the population that was economically better off, contributing to more inequality in the empire long term. The emperor had extensive rights and considerable executive powers, able to influence the makeup and functioning of some of the most important institutions.

The first years immediately after independence were marked by a lot of instability and conflict. There was another rebellion in the northern provinces, originating from Pernambuco, that quickly spread over most of northern Brazil in July 1824. The main leader of the insurrection was Frei Caneca (Friar Mug—the clergyman had sold mugs during his childhood), who incited the rebels against the heavily centralized system put in place by the 1824 Constitution. The insurrectionists, mostly made up of wealthy landowners and businessmen of the northeast, announced the formation of an independent state called the Confederation of the Equator, which would include Pernambuco, Paraíba, and Ceará.

The confederation was short-lived, however. The imperial forces subdued the rebels by November, executing the leaders. Though the rebellion was unsuccessful, the strong regional identity of Pernambuco and other northeastern territories of Brazil had manifested once again, and revolutionary sentiments would not immediately die down after 1824.

Another rebellion in the southern part of Brazil eventually forced the new empire into a conflict with the Argentinian United Provinces of the River Plate over the Cisplatina province. Conflict over the control of this land had long characterized Spanish-Portuguese relations, and it would end in a complete military defeat of the Brazilians in August 1828. The Brazilian army was disorganized and weak compared to the Argentinian forces, comprised of forcefully conscripted Brazilians and many foreign mercenaries. Both sides heavily suffered from the conflict that lasted over two years. Finally, a peace treaty was signed thanks to Britain's mediation, and the new independent nation of Uruguay emerged.

These conflicts highlighted some of the issues of the Brazilian economy, which was dealt a heavy blow that resulted in a full-blown financial crisis. The Bank of Brazil, opened in 1808 with the arrival of Dom João VI, was forced to close in 1829, as its gold reserves were completely depleted. Brazilian currency was devalued to fight against inflation but to no avail. Paper money that was issued was largely only valuable in Rio de Janeiro, whereas other major urban centers accepted it at a lower value, causing its value to fall further in relation to international currencies such as the British pound. This, in turn, caused problems with paying civil servants and members of the military, who were becoming increasingly critical of the regime. Anti-emperor liberal sentiments were on the rise in the second half of the 1820s.

The economic crisis was accompanied by a series of events that, when combined with the toll of war, caused widespread social upheaval in Brazil. With the death of Dom João VI of Portugal in 1826, Emperor Pedro was the next in line for the throne. There was serious concern in Brazil that he might bring back the union with Portugal and leave Rio for Lisbon. Dom Pedro, however, abdicated the Portuguese throne in favor of his daughter Maria. Since she was too young at the time to take over, his brother, Miguel, became the king. In the minds of the Brazilians, this decision was very telling. They believed their emperor should have renounced his ties to the Portuguese throne once and for all and established a new dynasty for Brazil. Still, this decision could not have reversed the economic and socio-political troubles experienced by the Brazilians.

The existing tensions in Brazilian society escalated from 1830 on, once again influenced by the changing situation in Europe, where a liberal revolution in France led to the establishment of the July Monarchy. Liberals all around the world were inspired to push for reforms, especially in such unequal societies in Brazil, where most of the population was excluded from such basic rights as voting in elections.

Brazilian newspapers started publishing prominent liberal manifestoes, and Rio de Janeiro was swept up with calls for the removal of the emperor from office. Adding to the turmoil were demonstrations of support from Portuguese royalists, who supported Emperor Pedro's position. This further angered the liberals, who were in the majority. In March 1831, several prominent military officials sided with the liberals, who demanded reforms. Facing mounting pressure and unable to resolve the situation, Dom Pedro I was forced to abdicate in April 1831 in favor of his son, Pedro II. Unbeknownst to the people of Brazil, this decision would lead to one of the most troubled times in Brazilian history known as the regency period, placing the future of the nation was in uncertain hands.

Chapter Four – From Empire to Republic

The Regency

The regency period was one of the most troubled decades in Brazilian history. In hindsight, it acted as a transitional period from the abdication of Emperor Pedro I in 1831 to the accession of his son, Pedro II (who was just five years old in 1831) in 1840. During this time, Brazil was ruled by a succession of different groups of politicians who tried to maintain order amidst uncertainty and crisis.

Ultimately, the regency period highlighted some of the most entrenched problems of the Brazilian socio-political sphere. Left without the "supervising" force of the emperor, who was an essential part of the still-young Brazilian state, the politicians in power fell victim to an array of conflicting interest groups that left the empire on the brink of collapse. Brazil was faced with serious domestic issues, stemming from the long-standing differences between its social classes and regional identities. Several important rebellions took place, claiming the lives of thousands of people in different parts of the empire as the regents were desperate to uphold their authority in the absence of the emperor.

Most of the measures implemented during the regency were aimed at reforming important aspects of Brazilian society, with the overarching goal of reducing centralized power. In June 1831, the Legislative General Assembly elected three individuals as regents in what is commonly referred to as the triumviral regency. The delegates were chosen to also act as representatives of different regions and interest groups: José de Costa Carvalho, a veteran politician and the founder of one of the most prominent newspapers in São Paulo, *O Farol Paulistano*; João Bráulio Muniz from Maranhão, representing the northern and northeastern regions; and Francisco de Lima e Silva, a military officer from Rio de Janeiro.

The "triumvirate" soon began its work, and one of its chief goals was to limit the extent of the moderating powers of the emperor. The Moderating Power was a special branch of power outlined by the 1824 Constitution that was exclusive to Brazil and vested considerable influence in the hands of the emperor. It was used to refer to the special competencies of the emperor, such as his constitutional right to freely appoint and dismiss ministers, convene the General Assembly or dissolve the Chamber of Deputies, veto proposed legislation, and grant amnesty or pardons to prisoners. Overall, as the name suggests, the emperor was to make decisions of such importance based on his judgment, as he was seen as an individual who stood above the state.

With the Additional Act of 1834, the regency proposed changes to the Constitution that were ultimately adopted by the largely liberal Chamber of Deputies, which had called for more decentralization of power. The Additional Act prohibited the use of the Moderating Power and granted provinces a larger amount of autonomy with the newly implemented regional legislative assemblies, which replaced the preceding General Councils (*Conselhos Gerais*). The assemblies had extensive rights to preside over local judicial and civil affairs without directly involving the central government. They could collect taxes, determine their budgets, and, perhaps most importantly, appoint civil servants in local positions.

The Additional Act also dissolved the Council of State (the exclusive advisory body that could be summoned by the emperor), which the legislators saw as largely useless. Rio de Janeiro was also changed into a Neutral Municipality, becoming an independent federal district, similar to Washington, D.C., in the United States. The influence of American federalism can clearly be seen in other reforms adopted during the regency period, such as the changes applied to the criminal justice code in 1832. These changes amplified the importance of the jury system for many court cases, similar to the American justice system.

Another important reform that preceded the adoption of the Additional Act was the creation of the National Guard—a measure to reform the disorganized Brazilian army, which had just suffered a defeat. Though it still contained many Portuguese-born officers in higher positions, the army's main problems were with ordinary soldiers at the bottom ranks, who had long complained of inadequate pay and poor conditions. The implementation of the National Guard aimed to diminish the importance of the centrally controlled imperial army, where most of the problems existed. Starting in 1831, all twenty-one to sixty-year-old males were required to enlist in regional National Guard regiments that essentially granted the provinces control over better-organized militias. Once enlisted, they were exempt from the imperial army draft. The main goal of the reform, influenced by similar measures adopted in France at the time, was to encourage the local citizens to actively participate in military affairs.

In 1835, elections were held to choose the sole regent who would take over for the triumviral regency that had ruled Brazil since 1831. This had been decided with the Additional Act one year earlier. The consensus since the beginning was that the triumvirate would not last until the accession of Pedro II. Diogo Antônio Feijó, a moderate liberal, became the new regent. Previously, he had served as the minister of justice and had advocated for more authority and decentralization.

During his time as the sole regent, Feijó was opposed by the conservative legislators, many of whom wanted Pedro I to return as the emperor, as well as the "exalted" radical liberal members, many of whom had advocated for the imperium's abolition and the establishment of a federal republic. Feijó was supposed to act as a mediator between the two groups and push moderate liberal reforms that would maintain the status quo of the constitutional monarchy, though he began to experience widespread opposition. More importantly, his tenure as the regent was plagued with provincial instability and the outbreak of two insurrections that would last well beyond the regency period: the Cabanagem in the province of Pará and the "Ragamuffin War" in Rio Grande do Sul in the south. We will cover the nature of these rebellions later, but they significantly weakened the position of Feijó, who faced strict criticism from his rivals for not being able to swiftly pacify the rebels. Eventually, in 1838, he was forced to resign. New elections were held, which were won by the conservative Pedro de Araújo Lima—the last of the regents of the transitory period.

Accession of Pedro II

Even before 1835, the regency had been troubled with several instances of armed uprisings in different parts of Brazil. Though these insurrections had no common agenda, they were all manifestations of strong regional positions against the moderate liberal status quo ushered in by the triumviral regency.

The uprisings were caused by a diverse set of factors. For example, the Cabanada rebellion, which broke out in Pernambuco in 1832, was largely a movement of the rural populations, who had suffered from the economic crisis caused by the decline of sugar and cotton prices. These people, known as the *cabanos*, comprised the lower echelons of northern and northeastern Brazilian society and advocated for the return of Dom Pedro I as the emperor. Though they were pacified in 1835, the *cabanos*, joined with the local Amerindians, slaves, and the mixed population of the region, also revolted in Belem, beginning another uprising known as the Cabanagem that lasted until 1840. Among the immediate causes of this insurrection, which decimated northern Brazil and an estimated fifth of the province's population, was the central government's appointment of a disfavored provincial president.

Salvador also became a center of popular uprisings, one of which was the slave rebellion of 1835 known as the Malê revolt. About 600 Malês, who constituted the Muslim slave minority of the city, rose up and caused chaos in Salvador. Government forces brutally suppressed the slaves in just a day due to the disorganized nature of the uprising, producing mixed responses from the opposing socio-political groups in Brazil. The Malê revolt of 1835 revived a debate about the practice of slavery in Brazil, which would become a prominent topic until the late years of the Brazilian Empire. Several other slave revolts would also break out in cities with large slave populations, such as Rio de Janeiro, though most failed because of the incoherence of the rebels' actions.

Also important was the insurrection known as the Sabinada (1837-1838), named after one of its leaders, Francisco Sabino. The Sabinada gained support from the middle class of Salvador but was eventually suppressed after a siege from the imperial forces that resulted in up to 2,000 casualties. Additionally, inhabitants of the state of Maranhão, who believed that they had been economically disadvantaged by the ongoing financial crisis, rose up in the 1838 revolt of the Balaiada, supported by some urban liberals. They gained control of the city of Caxias and caused widespread destruction for the next three years before being defeated by imperial forces in 1841.

In the southern lands of Rio Grande do Sul, the local *farrapos*, or "the people dressed in rags," revolted in 1835. The longest-lasting of the rebellions of the regency period (until 1845), the Farroupilha Revolt is also referred to as the Ragamuffin War. The leaders of this uprising were mostly wealthy cattle ranchers who had enjoyed close relations with the neighboring Uruguayans since colonial times and protested increased taxes on their province. The rebellion, thanks to great leadership from experienced revolutionaries—like the exiled Italian commander and future leader of Italy's unification, Giuseppe Garibaldi—was a thorn in the side of the Brazilian government. Soon, influenced by its Argentinian and Uruguayan ties, the revolt developed into a separatist movement, with the rebels proclaiming the de-facto independent Riograndense Republic and vigorously defending their position during the regency period.

In short, despite efforts to address some of the issues that had stemmed from the centralization of the Brazilian Empire, the regency experienced widespread problems that put a lot of pressure on the acting government, especially in the second half of the 1830s. Meanwhile, the Brazilian political spectrum was consumed by a firmer divide between liberals and conservatives, which would eventually result in the establishment of the two main political parties in the country.

After the conservative Araujo Lima assumed the position of regent, he proceeded to pass "regressive" measures to further centralize power. Among his regressionist policies was the rolling back of some of the provincial privileges implemented by the Additional Act of 1834. This caused discontent among the liberals but did not change the overall situation for the better. As the tensions continued, political elites began to increasingly favor the accession of the still-too-young Pedro II, who was only fourteen at the time.

The idea of lowering the age for accession to the throne had existed as early as during the first stage of the regency. Despite the liberal-conservative divide, one thing that both sides (except for radical advocates of republicanism) agreed on was the importance of the emperor. The elites knew that the regency was a transitory stage until the young heir to the throne came of age, after which the Brazilian political system would resume as outlined in the 1824 Constitution. The politicians respected the emperor and what the title stood for, largely acknowledging that the monarchy was an indispensable part of Brazil.

Thus, as Brazil's leaders struggled to deal with the ongoing crises, they decided to put their trust in the figure they believed possessed enough authority and respect to lead Brazil back to stability. The option of Pedro I returning as the emperor was no longer on the table, as he had passed away in Portugal in 1834. The next logical option was the young Pedro II.

Interestingly, it was the liberals who presented the legislation that proposed lowering the age of accession to the throne, setting in motion an active campaign to convince the legislators to pass it. Both chambers were eventually convinced. Having gained approval from the parliament, Dom Pedro II ascended to the throne of Brazil in July 1840.

The Second Reign

In hindsight, perhaps no one could have expected the extent of Brazil's transformation during the tenure of Pedro II as emperor, which lasted until 1889 and is referred to as the Second Reign. When he ascended the throne in 1840, the fourteen-year-old Pedro II's empire was experiencing a severe economic crisis, high levels of social inequality, and an ongoing rebellion in the south. Throughout his reign, Brazil emerged as arguably the most powerful nation in South America with a modernized economy and a fundamentally transformed social system. This fifty-nine-year period brought a series of socio-cultural developments that provided the basis of Brazilian life during the twentieth century. Most remarkably, the prominent social and political groups inside Brazil, despite their many differences, got to work to solve the most pressing of Brazil's problems and put the nation on a path toward progress by the end of the century.

The first few years of Pedro II's reign were marked by a continuation of the "regressive" measures initiated by the conservative leaders before his accession, which put considerable power back into the hands of the monarch. The political elites were largely in agreement that strengthening the power of the emperor was the first step toward progress. Many of the emperor's competencies, bestowed on him by the constitutional Moderating Power, were brought back. This was balanced with the implementation of a "reverse" parliamentarian model in 1847, creating the position of President of the Council of Ministers. The emperor would choose the president, who would essentially act as the head of the government. This position was something like the role of a prime minister in most parliamentarian systems. According to the changes, the president of the Council of Ministers would choose the respective ministers. The Council of Ministers held executive power but needed the trust of both the emperor and the Chamber of Deputies to function.

This was a unique way of dividing the different branches of power in Brazil, with the emperor enjoying a privileged position with his Moderating Power—which made the Brazilian system not fully "parliamentary in the modern sense of the word. Interestingly, this system ensured that the government's makeup was constantly modified and the cabinet was always composed of new ministers. This resulted in more than thirty different iterations of the government until 1889, and representatives from neither political party were excluded. The rapidly changing nature of the Brazilian government made it possible to avoid frequent confrontations about who truly held power. The system felt balanced and was largely unmodified.

These developments in Brazil's political sphere resulted in the entrenchment of a party system that became stable by the 1870s. The old liberal-conservative divide was still prevalent, though the new generation of politicians enjoyed the advantages of a more cohesive political system where both parties developed reasonable agendas and platforms. The emperor played the role of a neutral referee between the two camps, who rightfully considered each other rivals.

The entrenchment of the party system was manifested in the pronounced regional and social support obtained by the two parties by the end of the Second Reign. The conservatives were largely supported by the rich rural landowners and urban merchants from the provinces of Pernambuco and Bahia, the old centers of the Brazilian political and economic sphere. They advocated for the protection of regional economic interests and a strong central government. The liberals, on the other hand, found the main bases of their support in the southern provinces of São Paulo, Minas Gerais, and Rio Grande do Sul.

Important improvements were made to the country's economic structure, including changes to tariffs on imported goods. The Alves Branco Tariff, adopted in 1844, greatly increased customs duties on certain products, some to 30 percent and others as much as 60 percent. Thousands of imported goods were affected, to the dismay of foreign merchants—mostly the British, who largely held a monopoly in the Brazilian markets. The main goal of the policy was to encourage domestic production and local regional centers of manufacturing. Overall, it was a successful move that, paired with other changes aimed at modernization, aimed to make Brazil competitive with the rapidly industrializing Western nations of the nineteenth century.

Meanwhile, a product emerged that defined the socioeconomic situation of late nineteenth-century Brazil: coffee. Introduced to Brazil in the 1720s and first planted in Rio de Janeiro and the surrounding areas in the 1760s, coffee quickly became a pillar of Brazil's export economy. The Paraiba Valley provided an excellent place to grow coffee, becoming a staple of the region despite the difficulties of its harvesting. Dependent on slave labor, the growth of the Brazilian coffee industry coincided with the increasing demand for coffee in European and North American markets. By 1890, coffee made up about 60 percent of Brazil's export economy.

The coffee planters eventually accrued tremendous power in Brazilian society, emerging as the "coffee bourgeoisie" and providing the basis for the later republican developments in the country. The concentration of coffee production in the southern region also resulted in the cementing this part of Brazil as the socioeconomic center of the country. Early after colonization, the northeastern region had been most important because it was where sugar production was the most advanced. With the increased prevalence of coffee as the main product of the Brazilian economy, the southern part of the country once and for all wrestled this title away from the northeast.

The slave question became increasingly prominent during the Second Reign. Slavery in its many different forms had been abolished in the most advanced European societies, which were starting to embrace the principles of classical liberalism. Britain had been a leading force in the end of the Atlantic Slave Trade—a practice started by the Portuguese during colonial times, as you may remember. The British gave themselves the right to inspect any ships in the Atlantic that were suspected of transporting slaves, greatly accelerating the end of the slave trade. By the late 1860s, the last major Western society—the United States—had also abolished slavery.

In contrast to all these developments, the Brazilian economy still largely depended on slavery, with most slaves employed on the coffee plantations of the Paraiba Valley. Rio de Janeiro had a significant number of slaves, as well, with slaves constituting roughly 40 percent of the population.

Thus, the slavery issue was hotly contested among the Brazilians. With coffee becoming a central part of the Brazilian economy, many were against the abolition of slavery, which they believed posed an economic threat. The emperor, on the other hand, had abolitionist tendencies. He had publicly criticized slavery in Brazil on several occasions and was one of the main advocates for gradual reform instead of immediate abolition.

In 1850, a law was adopted by the Chamber of Deputies and passed in the Senate that recognized ships that transported slaves as participants in piracy. This was directly influenced by similar British legislation, the Aberdeen Act, which imprisoned slave traffickers in the Atlantic and tried them in British courts. The adopted measures and more active British involvement resulted in the quick decline and eventual end of the slave trade from Africa into Brazilian ports by the late 1850s.

A logical follow-up to the end of the slave trade would be the abolition of the practice in Brazil for good. Yet again, though everyone (especially the political elite on both flanks) acknowledged that abolition was inevitable, there were disagreements on how to implement it. Most began to agree that a gradual abolition was the way to go. A factor that played a decisive role in the decision was the immigration of large numbers of Europeans to Brazil during the middle of the nineteenth century.

Lawmakers realized that the immigrants arriving in Brazil in increasing numbers could replace the labor of slaves. They began working on policies to guarantee the immigrants did not emerge as an economically dominant class themselves and compete against the landowners, who would be deprived of slave labor. This was in the government's best interests. The rich landowners were, realistically, the backbone of the Brazilian economy. Granted, the way they had gotten rich—by relying on slave labor—was immoral, but something had to be done. International pressure was mounting, and the public was aware of the abolitionist sympathies of the emperor.

The Land Act (Landed Property Act), adopted in 1850 soon after the ban on the slave trade, served exactly this purpose. Its main goal was to legalize the rural properties of the landowners, most of whom had acquired public lands long before through government grants. The law required the landowners to register their estates. Additionally, and more importantly, the law asserted that immigrants could not buy land for three years after coming to Brazil. This was crucial in convincing many of the richest landowners to support abolition. At the least, it provided a foundation for later abolitionist measures.

The government did not want the positive economic trends Brazil had been experiencing for the past few years to stop. It looked to some of the most developed nations for inspiration and noticed a crucial factor that had boosted industrialization in places like Britain and the United States. The obvious and easily implementable answer lay in modernizing the country's infrastructure. Modernity, in the nineteenth century, was associated with railways, which facilitated the inter- and intra-regional transportation of goods, labor, and the military. Thus, rail lines were built throughout the country, linking important centers like Recife with Salvador in the northeast and the inland points of southern coffee production with Rio de Janeiro. Several highways were also constructed to improve the overall transportation system.

Many of the infrastructural projects were made possible thanks to British investments, though a significant number were financed with the revenue accrued by the state through the Alves Branco tariff. Perhaps the most important early industrial businessman in Brazil was Irineu Evangelista de Souza, the Viscount of Mauá, whose investments contributed to the development of the country's infrastructural and financial systems.

With major improvements to modernization and industrialization, the government made a conscious choice to focus on attracting European immigrants as an alternative to slaves. Something that explains this decision was the prejudice of most white Brazilians against African slaves, influenced by the Social Darwinist theories of the nineteenth century that provided a pseudo-scientific justification for European imperialism. If slaves were freed, the landowners would not regard them as equals, and, as was the case, widespread discrimination in their working environments would continue.

Still, in the early 1850s, certain landowners had experimented with an immigrant workforce, such as Senator Nicolau Vergueiro, who first brought Swiss and German immigrant farmers to his coffee plantations. However, the newly arrived Europeans were subject to exploitation and harsh working conditions, which they were not used to in Europe. They soon expressed their discontent and left Vergueiro's estates.

It was not until the 1870s that the government began to actively encourage the immigration of foreign workers. This was because the influx of new slaves from Africa had almost fully stopped and the slaves who remained on the plantations were rapidly aging, affecting coffee production. The government discussed the possible policies with the landowners and passed laws that helped foreigners better integrate into Brazil, for example by subsidizing their passage into the country. São Paulo became the center of European immigration, with more than 10,000 registered immigrants legally moving to the city by 1880.

Many Europeans still found the conditions offered by Brazil to be very difficult to adapt to, spreading unfavorable news of the situation back to their home countries. The Brazilian government combatted this by issuing propaganda pamphlets in European societies like Italy and Germany, which were undergoing massive socio-economic shifts. In these pamphlets, they advertised the opportunities in Brazil in contrast to other major immigrant destinations, such as the United States. Italians were especially targeted, as the country had completed its political unification in the 1870s, accelerating industrialization and switching to a capitalist economy. This had left many of the poorer classes disadvantaged, with more incentives to search for new opportunities overseas.

Thus, in the final decade of the Brazilian Empire, immigration numbers began to drastically increase, reaching their peak during the first decades of the twentieth century. By 1888, São Paulo housed as many as 100,000 immigrants, the vast majority of whom were Italians.

Meanwhile, abolitionists began to rise in prominence in the urban centers of Brazil, founding different groups where they discussed the future of Brazilian society. These groups spread pamphlets and manifestos all around Brazil, convincing much of the population that slavery must be abandoned for good.

With the slave population rapidly shrinking to only about 5 percent of Brazil's population by the late 1880s, the slavery debate was reheated. By then, the immigrant attraction policies had also demonstrated their success. The Brazilian legislators began to work on the issue in the spring of 1888. They were motivated by Princess Isabel, the daughter of Pedro II, who delivered a powerful speech demonstrating the backwardness of slavery and its incompatibility with the modern society Brazil was striving toward. In May 1888, a bill on the abolition of slavery, known as the Golden Law, was drafted and quickly adopted with overwhelming support from both chambers of the National Congress. Brazil thus became the last of the major Latin American colonies to abolish slavery, paving the way for the republican era of the country's history.

In addition to the extensive transformation of the socioeconomic aspects of Brazilian life, one of the main achievements of Pedro II's reign was the reorganization of the military. The National Guard was reformed so that its leaders were chosen by the central government and its appointees in the provinces, and its roles were modified to balance the institution with the imperial army. This measure was adopted in the first half of the 1840s, making it possible for the Brazilian army to gain a significant advantage against the rebels in the south.

As we mentioned, Pedro II had inherited a separatist rebellion in the south, but the imperial government negotiated with the rebels in 1845 instead of continuing the war effort. The self-declared Riograndense Republic was dissolved and rejoined Brazil in exchange for amnesty for the rebels and greater provincial autonomy.

In 1848—the year of liberal revolutions throughout Europe—Brazil experienced the Praieira rebellion in Pernambuco, influenced by the radical republican and socialist ideas of thinkers like Fourier. The rebels caused instability in Recife and the surrounding areas but never accrued enough support to pose a threat to the reorganized Brazilian military. The rebellion was largely pacified soon after it broke out, but pockets of rebel fighters engaged in guerilla tactics until 1850. The Praieira revolt marked the final of the insurrections in Pernambuco, which had historically been prone to such movements. Throughout the reign of Pedro II, no more major revolts broke out in the northeast.

Finally, Pedro II's reign was memorable because of Brazil's successful involvement in a series of conflicts over disputes among the newly independent South American nations. The region had been rather unstable since the beginning of the nineteenth century, and we already mentioned some of the conflicts the Brazilian Empire had to get involved in.

In 1851, the governor of Buenos Aires—Juan Manuel de Rosas—had accrued too much power in Argentina and set his eyes on the ongoing

Uruguayan Civil War. Rosas, trying to exploit the chaos and dominate the former territories of the Spanish Viceroyalty of the Rio de la Plata, supported the nationalist Blanco Party. A potential victory for Rosas would greatly endanger Brazil's interests in the region and lead to further destabilization, so Pedro II decided to intervene. Brazil provided support for the Uruguayan liberal Colorado Party and entered the civil war, also gaining support from Argentinian provinces that had been upset with Rosas' authority. After five months of fighting, Brazil and its allies prevailed, ousting Rosas. The belligerents returned to the status quo, which only increased Brazilian influence in the south.

In August 1864, when Uruguay was plunged into deep political turmoil yet again, Pedro II's representatives presented an ultimatum to the two parties, as the civil war had endangered the safety of Brazilian Natives residing in Uruguay. The Brazilian emperor had demanded a ceasefire and threatened to intervene if denied. Ultimately, the imperial army had to intervene again on behalf of the liberal Colorado Party, though the government at the time never acknowledged official involvement in the war. By February 1865, the Blanco Party was overwhelmed due to the pressure put on its possessions by the Brazilian-Colorado forces, eventually capitulating and ending the conflict. The short conflict was another great political victory for Pedro II's Brazil, as well as for Argentine President Bartolomé Mitre, who had expressed his support for the Colorado Party.

However, the Uruguayan War indirectly led to another conflict—the largest war between states in South American history. Paraguay's nationalist President Francisco Solano Lopez had supported the Blanco faction in Uruguay and was devastated after their defeat at the hands of Brazil. Motivated by imperialist designs, he had denounced Brazil's involvement in the Uruguayan Civil War repeatedly throughout the mid-months of 1864 and had threatened to act. Action materialized in November, as Brazilian forces were still occupied by the war in Uruguay. Paraguayan forces, numbering as many as 80,000 men, crossed into Brazilian territory, forcing Brazil's imperial forces to mobilize against an invasion.

While the initial Paraguayan invasion was repelled, President Lopez also ordered an invasion of Argentine territories that had been disputed between the two countries. This essentially forced Brazil and Argentina into the Treaty of the Triple Alliance with their recent ally Uruguay in May 1865. The combined forces of the alliance proved too difficult for the Paraguayans, who were already struggling by the end of the year. In 1866, the veteran Marquess of Caxias, Lima e Silva from Brazil, assumed command, resulting in a series of victories for the allied forces, who took control of Paraguay's capital, Asuncion, in late 1868. President Lopez fled the city, organizing his forces into guerilla fighting bands. He put up a fight for the next two years before his death during the Battle of Cerro Cora in March 1870.

Above all, the war had a devastating effect on Paraguay. Not only did it lose all its territorial claims, but its population suffered immensely from the conflict. Certain estimates place Paraguayan casualties as high as 200,000, including civilians and soldiers who died from causes associated with the war, like hunger and disease. Brazilian forces remained in Paraguay until 1876, overseeing the creation of a pro-Brazilian government in Asuncion.

Ultimately, because of Brazil's success in these Platine Wars during the 1850s and through the late 1860s, the nation emerged as a dominant force in South America and the Western Hemisphere. Nevertheless, the war brought to the forefront many problems that eventually became troublesome to Pedro II and his government.

The Death of the Empire

The reign of Pedro II ended abruptly in November of 1889, and with it came the dissolution of the Empire of Brazil. It all transpired quickly, with a coup d'état organized by some of the highest-ranking military officers in Brazil forcing the emperor to abdicate. Pedro II obliged without resistance. By the morning of November 16, the Republic of Brazil was proclaimed, with former marshal Deodoro da Fonseca as the interim president of the provisional government until the new political system could be fully adopted.

But what were those behind the coup aiming for? Why had they been dissatisfied with Pedro II's rule?

We already mentioned some of the key areas in which Brazil experienced significant advancements during the long reign of Pedro II. The emperor had struck a comfortable balance between the main political parties of the empire and established a stable system since his accession as a fourteen-year-old. Brazil's economy had grown considerably, and so had its population—reaching about 14,000,000 people by the late 1880s. The nation had made considerable efforts to modernize by improving networks of communication and infrastructure to better connect its vast lands. Geopolitically, Brazil had managed to eclipse virtually all the nations of South America, having emerged victorious from the many conflicts in the south. With an influx of new workers in the form of foreign immigrants, increased urbanization, and normalized relations with European nations, it certainly seemed on the surface that the future of the empire was in safe hands. In fact, since the end of the Paraguayan War, the Brazilian economy had undergone a noticeable shift that favored a new emerging middle class.

However, recent reforms and socio-political developments had left many dissatisfied, not to mention other factors contributing to adverse sentiments against the emperor.

First, those close to the emperor noticed his increasing lack of enthusiasm for fulfilling his duties as emperor. The ailing emperor with poor health was disfavored by the new generation of Brazilian politicians, who had matured during the age of Brazil's progress. The older generation, which had regarded the institute of the emperor as essential to the Brazilian state, were slowly being replaced by new faces that were critical of the emperor and his role.

In addition, Pedro II had lived through the deaths of two of his sons and potential heirs. This had proved especially difficult for the mental state of the emperor, who began to disfavor his daughter, Isabel, as a potential successor to the throne. Although the accession of a woman was not technically impossible, Emperor Pedro believed that only a man could bear a burden as heavy as being the emperor of Brazil. This led to his pessimistic attitudes that could no longer bear the scrutiny of some of his main political rivals.

Pedro II.'

Forces in the social and political spheres of Brazil accelerated the decline of Pedro II's regime. One such group was the rich landowners who had largely been left dissatisfied with the abolition of slavery. They had to adapt to the new circumstances and increase their expenditures, even though their revenues were still very high.

The regime had also quarreled with the Catholic Church—one of the pillars of the Brazilian state and the official religion. According to the Constitution, however, the Church operated under the authority of Pedro II, not the pope from the Vatican. This meant that all decisions regarding the organization or operation of Church activities had to go through the emperor before being implemented in Brazil. From the mid-1870s, several prominent bishops had begun to defy imperial authority in hopes of more autonomy.

Similar sentiments had existed in the military, with some of the highest-ranking officers believing that they were undervalued despite their successes in Brazil's many wars. They had long voiced their desire for more autonomy in the army's affairs, which was also strictly controlled by the government. Ordinary soldiers were not getting enough pay or promotions to keep up with the rapidly modernizing economy of the country, feeling unjustly disadvantaged.

Most importantly, however, the main drivers of the coup d'état were members of the republican movement. During the peak of European imperialism, only a handful of powerful nations in the industrialized world had democratic or republican systems—the United States and Great Britain being the chief examples. Brazil had been the only remaining monarchy in Latin America, where the former colonies had all switched to republican systems. Brazilian liberals had long been active in the country's politics, supporting a federalist reorganization of Brazil with more autonomous provinces.

Modernization and urbanization had increased liberal sentiments among members of the public, who began forming societies and clubs where they advocated for the establishment of a Brazilian republic. They saw a monarchic system with this much power and leverage as old-fashioned and pointed at the issue of slavery as a clear indication that it needed to be changed. In the eyes of the republicans, Brazil had been too slow to abolish slavery, and the gradual process had left some of the key groups dissatisfied. Modernity, for them, required an adequate political system where the diverse voices of the public would be justly considered, not one where certain individuals were clearly favored over others.

Brazilian republicans were the leaders behind the drive against the monarchy, and they were joined by other discontent groups by 1889 in voicing their concerns, most importantly the military. This unlikely alliance began to prepare its conspiracy against Pedro II after the adoption of the Golden Law in 1888. To the surprise of many, the rich conservative landowners joined the republican cause against the monarchy, which they believed was biased against them. Though they recouped their losses soon after the abolition of slavery, they were still upset at the emperor and wished to exact their revenge.

The Council of Ministers tried to enact measures during 1889 to please some of the most dissatisfied groups, led by its liberal President Afonso Celso de Assis Figueiredo, the Viscount of Ouro Preto. Among the reforms he had hoped to pass were universal suffrage, a reorganization of the imperial Senate and the National Guard to please the military, and more autonomy for the Brazilian provinces. However, the legislators refused to accept his reforms, further contributing to the anti-regime movements in the nation.

On November 15, 1889, the republican conspirators, joined by hundreds of soldiers and military officers, took to the streets of Rio and organized a swift coup d'état, arresting the Viscount of Ouro Preto (President of the Council of Ministers) and taking control of the government overnight. They were led by Marshal Deodoro de Fonseca, an old commander of the imperial army who had been convinced to join the insurrection days before. Before the coup was staged, the conspirators had spread rumors about a potential crackdown on individuals in the military with republican sentiments, further antagonizing the soldiers against the emperor.

Meanwhile, Pedro II decided to immediately return from his residence in Petropolis, hoping to stabilize the situation. He had believed that the insurrectionists were demanding the replacement of the existing Council of Ministers, and he thought he could pacify them if he elected a new cabinet. Upon his arrival, however, de Fonseca and others informed the emperor that they intended to end the monarchy. However, they stressed that they wanted to avoid a violent clash against forces loyal to the empire. Hearing the news, Pedro II decided not to resist, agreeing to abdicate and go into exile to Europe to avoid further chaos in the country. A new era in the history of Brazil had begun.

Chapter Five – The Struggles of the Brazilian Republic

República Velha

General Deodoro da Fonseca thus became the first president of the newly established republican regime in Brazil, ushering in about forty years commonly referred to as the *República Velha*, or "Old Republic." During these years, Brazil became a constitutional democracy with an elected president, navigating through the first decades of the volatile twentieth century. As is usually the case, the country experienced some of the most pressing challenges during this time, culminating with a revolution that overthrew the government in 1830. In this chapter, we will look at some of the major developments that took place during the First Brazilian Republic.

General Deodoro da Fonseca (1889).[8]

Resistance to the new political situation materialized as early as the first weeks after the proclamation of the republic in November 1889. In the next few days, there were several small-scale uprisings in the military, with monarchist battalions rising up against Fonseca. Rebellions broke out all over the country, including in Rio de Janeiro. The rebels mostly demanded the restoration of the emperor, though their movements were largely disorganized and could not achieve anything of significance.

By late 1890, the new regime had managed to pacify these uprisings, while the politicians in charge of the provisional government began constructing a new order in place of one enforced by Pedro II. Thus came the first republican constitution in February 1891, which officially declared Brazil a constitutional democracy.

Inspired by United States and Swiss federalism, the 1891 Constitution aimed to decentralize power by abolishing the Moderating Power entirely. Firstly, the country was renamed the Republic of the United States of Brazil. The old provinces were renamed "states," and their powers and competencies greatly increased. The National Congress (made up of the Chamber of Deputies and the Senate) was retained, though senators were no longer elected for life; their terms were fixed at nine years.

The executive branch of the government was headed by a president, who served for four years alongside a vice-president, who also acted as the president of the Senate. The two could not be reelected immediately following one term in office. They would be elected through a direct voting system, and voters would be required to provide signatures on their ballots. The old census voting, which had been based on the voters' income, was also abolished, and the voting age was changed to twenty-one. However, women, members of the clergy, soldiers, and the "illiterate and beggars" were excluded from voting.

Finally, the state and the Catholic Church were separated from each other, and the state would be unable to intervene in the affairs of the religious institution.

What did these constitutional changes mean for Brazil? It meant that despite all its claims, the new system was one of the most undemocratic constitutional democracies in the world at the time. The main problems were the restrictive voting conditions and the non-secret voting mechanism, which resulted in a series of essentially rigged elections. In what became known as *coronelismo*, or the rule of the colonels, oligarchs in São Paulo, Minas Gerais, and Rio de Janeiro exercised great influence on the registered voters employed at their plantations, manipulating votes in their favor.

This resulted in the country successively being governed by governments formed by the local Paulista Republican Party (PRP) and the Meneiro (Minas Gerais) Republican Party (PRM). This highlighted the main problem of the republican movement in Brazil: it had not been a widespread popular movement. The elites behind the coup d'état of 1889 could not risk open elections, perhaps believing that the nation's voters would disfavor them.

The pitfalls of the established regime in Brazil began to show one by one. Soon after the adoption of the new constitution, the country was plunged back into an economic crisis. President de Fonseca caused widespread outrage when he wished to dissolve the National Congress to deal with the situation, leading to a naval revolt in Rio de Janeiro organized by one of the admirals of the Brazilian Navy. In November, fearing an escalation that could claim innocent lives, Deodoro de Fonseca resigned. Then-vice president Floriano Peixoto succeeded him in office. Peixoto had himself been an experienced army veteran and was similar minded to his predecessor, hoping to increase both his own powers and the role of the military in the nation's affairs.

The new president presided over some of the most volatile years of the Old Republic, forced to deal with the financial crisis caused by the unregulated development of the Brazilian financial sector since the mid-nineteenth century. His inability to deal with the problems caused by the collapse of the economy, including high levels of inflation, led to the breakout of another naval revolt in March 1893. This time, the revolt escalated into a conflict between forces loyal to the government and rebels. It ended in Peixoto's victory the following year after he had authorized the purchase of foreign warships with state funds.

All this added up to cause another revolt—the Federalist Revolution, which was launched in February 1893. This movement was not ideologically homogenous, consisting of not only radical republicans and advocates of federalism left dissatisfied by the adopted political system but also monarchists who aimed to restore the empire. Some of the rebels were also motivated to rise against the powerful governor of the Rio Grande do Sul—Júlio de Castilhos—who they believed abused his powers. The rebels were finally pacified in 1895 after they joined forces with the naval mutineers, who were also defeated by the government forces. In total, their clashes with the Brazilian army resulted in an estimated 10,000 casualties, further destabilizing the southern part of the nation.

Only in March 1894 were the first presidential elections held in Brazil, resulting in the election of Prudente de Morais—the first president of the country not from a military background. An experienced lawyer and politician, de Morais had served as the governor of São Paulo. He was the first of the succeeding "coffee" presidents from Minas Gerais, which dominated Brazilian politics until 1930.

President Morais further reinforced the concentration of power in the hands of the rich southern elite. Most of them were coffee planters, and coffee exports reached all-time highs in the history of the Brazilian economy. This completed the enduring shift of the socio-political center of Brazil from the north to the south, but it came with severe consequences. Brazil became overly reliant on coffee as its main export, and its agricultural specter almost ignored other plants that could be grown. This meant that Brazil had to import most of its foodstuffs from its neighbors or overseas. Eventually, when the price of coffee decreased in the international market, so did the economic situation of Brazilian coffee planters. The planters lobbied the government to artificially inflate international coffee prices by buying it from the market. This practice began in 1906 and lasted for several years, but soon the government realized that it could not be sustained long-term, and its negative tolls began to show on the Brazilian economy.

Fall of the Old Republic

The domination of Minas Gerais and São Paulo in Brazilian politics resulted in the two regional republican parties constantly winning elections. The parties developed a mutual understanding that gave them a massive comparative political advantage over their northern or northeastern rivals, who could not amass the same resources to contest the elections. This period of southern political supremacy came to be referred to as *café com leite* or "coffee with milk" politics, referring to the two most important industries of the regions—coffee for São Paulo and dairy for Minas Gerais. The nickname also stems from the fact that the two regions cooperated for decades to push their agendas in the domestic political sphere, largely neglecting the problems faced by other regions of Brazil. The socio-economic and political vitality of the south, especially of São Paulo, was thus finally cemented at the expense of the north.

Despite the eventual plunge of coffee prices in the early twentieth century and the disruption of the Brazilian economy, the number of immigrants coming to the country only increased, contributing to the growth of urban centers such as São Paulo. The city soon began to eclipse Rio de Janeiro in almost all respects. By 1910, the city's population had increased to about 400,000 people—a tenfold increase from about 40,000 people in 1885. Santos, a nearby port city, attracted increasing traffic as the main route of export from São Paulo, resulting in its enrichment. In the north, the discovery of rubber in the Amazonas state contributed to the development and urbanization of the region as well, with the city of Manaus becoming a new center.

Rapid urbanization also brought its own problems. For instance, Rio de Janeiro suffered from sanitation and health problems, leading to regular outbreaks of diseases such as smallpox and yellow fever. When officials began implementing changes to the city's urban design and tried to combat the poor health situation in Rio by making vaccination mandatory in the fall of 1904, a large part of the population was outraged. Local soldiers, who had also been dissatisfied with the new republican regime, tried to mobilize the masses into a short rebellion in November known as the Vaccine Revolt, which was promptly suppressed by the government troops.

The pseudo-democratic political system implemented in the 1890s began to show cracks by the second decade of the twentieth century. The decentralized federalist system had resulted in a poorly integrated national economy where there were clear winners and losers. Urbanization, wherever it took place, had transpired without the emergence of a prominent middle class that would take an active part in the socio-political sphere of Brazil. Independent states with their own industries exported their products to foreign markets and largely neglected the domestic market. This contributed to the growth of regional rivalries and further accelerated the development of the more profitable south.

Connectedness between the vast territories of the nation should have been provided by an extensive road and railway network, but this was considered costly and was not favored by potential investors. The lack of advanced communication systems, such as telegraphs in remote areas, meant that it could take a few weeks for information to be transmitted from one place to another. The rich oligarch landowners, who had concentrated most of the nation's wealth in their hands, were not interested in better integrating the different Brazilian provinces to keep their status quo.

The Brazilian economy had also become too dependent on specialized agricultural production and had almost neglected industrialization, outside of certain reforms during the reign of Pedro II. This was partially a legacy of being the last American nation to abolish slavery. Without the prominence of local manufacturing, the country depended on the import of manufactured goods from European and North American markets. This contributed to the lack of technological development in Brazil's industries as well as agriculture, which decreased productivity.

What led to the emergence of social and political movements that eventually ended the oligarchic regime of the Old Republic was World War I. The outbreak of the war in 1914 reshaped the priorities of European nations, most importantly Britain, slowing the export of its manufactured goods to foreign markets.

The war, the deadliest in human history up to that time, not only put great pressure on the economies of the belligerents but also indirectly affected the situation elsewhere. Brazil experienced another severe crisis and inflation caused by the drop in coffee's demand and prices around the world and the government's efforts to subsidize local producers.

With coffee production plummeting, those who had worked for the planters began to join the urban middle and working classes, resulting in a surprising increase in the domestic production of manufactured goods. Brazilian factories produced goods that were cheaper in the domestic market, and the domestic flow of capital began to finally increase as the coffee oligarchs struggled to maintain their domination. The disruption of the import of foodstuffs also created a demand for the diversification of Brazilian agriculture, though coffee and sugar were never ousted as the primary export goods.

With the influx of foreign immigrants from Europe during and after the war years, prominent political ideologies of the time—most importantly anarchism and socialism—were on the rise. Widespread dissatisfaction with the country's socio-economic and political situation was increasingly voiced. People began to realize that the status quo favored only a handful of individuals, while the great potential of the country was not being utilized by the government, which was dominated by the interests of the oligarchs.

The emerging urban middle class formed a loose alliance with factory workers, industrialists, and people employed in the public sector, advocating for reforms after the First World War. Their demands ranged from the implementation of universal suffrage to a reformation of the educational system, the industrialization of the nation, and the improvement of workers' conditions.

Anti-government sentiments were shared by some of the army officers and, together, these groups formed a coalition for the 1922 presidential elections. Despite their best efforts, they lost, and the PRM retained the oligarchic status quo. The disappointing result became the subject of a protest in Rio, where some members of the military launched an unsuccessful rebellion.

This began an eight-year struggle between the government and its southern oligarchic supporters and dissidents who criticized the regime, led by junior military officers—the *tenentes*. The *tenentes* did not give up their hopes of forcing the government to pass national reforms that would consider the interests of most of the population. Over the next few years, they were a thorn in the government's side, organizing minor rebellions all over the country. Their efforts of resistance increased nationalist sentiments among the public, which began to increasingly mobilize against the government.

The Vargas Era

On October 29, 1929, with the United States stock market crash, Brazil was plunged into the Great Depression. Coffee prices plummeted once again on the international market as different nations tried to combat the inflation and unemployment caused by the financial crisis. Brazil's government, as before, tried to artificially manipulate coffee prices to guarantee a reliable stream of income for the coffee planters, who had become more and more dependent on the interventionist policies of favorable politicians. However, as is usually the case in an economic crisis, the middle and lower classes were hit the hardest, adding to their discontent and pushing the tensions to new highs ahead of the 1930 presidential elections.

A heterogeneous alliance of the middle and working classes, *tenentes*, industrialists, and socialists was formed in 1929. It nominated Getúlio Vargas as its representative against the Paulista nominee Julio Prestes for the 1930 elections.

Vargas had himself come from a family of landowners from Rio Grande do Sul, earning his name among the political actors of the 1920s. He recognized the fundamental problems Brazil faced, and his platform included promises about industrialization, nationalization of the country's resources, the extension of voting rights, and reformation of the federalist system.

Throughout the years, he had accrued enough political clout from the dissatisfied groups within the country to emerge as essentially a populist leader, claiming that the "real people" had been disadvantaged by a group of corrupt elites—something that resonated deeply with the public.

For the 1930 elections, he had strategically chosen João Pessoa from the northeastern Paraiba region as his running mate, exploiting the long regional rivalry of Brazil. As he campaigned extensively before the elections, hopes were high that the political dominance of the southern coffee elite would once and for all be put to an end.

Getulio Vargas.⁹

The 1930 election, like most of the prior elections in Brazil, was plagued with widespread corruption and fraud, ending in the victory of Julio Prestes with 57 percent of the votes. Vargas had only been victorious in Rio Grande do Sul (with over 99 percent of the votes), Minas Gerais, and Paraiba, accruing a total of over 700,000 votes. He and his coalition refused to accept the results of the election, contributing to the rising tensions inside the country.

Crucially, in June of 1930, Joao Pessoa was murdered in Recife, sparking widespread protests and instability in the northeast that had to be dealt with by government forces. Vargas, having built an extensive network of contacts in the military sympathetic to his platform, began planning a conspiracy to seize power. The conspirators devised detailed plans to take over several of the country's most important locations, beginning their actions in early October of the same year before Prestes could enter office and begin his duties.

Revolutionary forces acted quickly and decisively, gaining the upper hand by the middle of the month, with Vargas publicly demonstrating his intentions. By October 24, President Washington Luis had been ousted, and a military junta was established in Rio to oversee the ceding of power. With the revolution of 1830, the Old Republic came to an end and the Vargas era began.

Starting in November 1930, Getúlio Vargas exercised full control over the political affairs of Brazil. The very first decisions taken by him and his supporters were aimed at depriving his political rivals of influence and centralizing power in the hands of the president. The obvious issue with Vargas and the broad alliance that had supported his ascent to power had been the lack of a cohesive program, something that was necessary if the new president wished to drag the country out of the recession caused by the Great Depression. Partly to give himself time to consolidate his position, Vargas repealed the 1891 Constitution, dissolved the main legislative bodies of the country, and assumed the leadership of a "provisional government" before a new constitution was enacted in 1934.

To address the country's dire economic circumstances, Vargas adopted a series of interventionist policies that granted tax breaks to certain groups, imposed import quotas on foreign goods, and encouraged the expansion of the domestic industrial sector. These policies, again, did not follow a sound economic or ideological agenda. Instead, they were mainly immediate efforts at consolidating support from the rising middle classes.

Importantly, Vargas linked his state interventionist policies and the necessity to industrialize with nationalism, publicly criticizing the influence of foreign actors on Brazil. The main interest group Vargas favored were the northeastern landowners, who had been a significant force in the coalition behind the new president. To repay for their support and take a jab at the influence of the southern coffee oligarchs, Vargas promoted the diversification of the country's agriculture in the northeast, reasserting their leverage on the workforce. This went against some of the more socialist promises of Vargas' platform. Rural workers became more disadvantaged, fueling the rise of leftist sentiments against the new ruler.

It thus became apparent early on that Vargas would continue to favor his supporters with his socio-economic measures and increase his political power through centralization. This led to several revolts against the new regime, most of which were promptly suppressed by local loyalist troops. The army under Vargas was also not afraid to use force against a wave of left-wing and student protests. In the summer of 1932, the dissatisfied southern coffee oligarchs launched the Constitutionalist Revolution to try and oust Vargas from power, resulting in up to 5,000 casualties. The revolt was sparked after government forces had killed four student activists in May, but the rebels could not amass enough support to seriously challenge Vargas' regime.

The attempted revolution made Vargas realize he could not move further toward his goals of centralization without catering to the coffee planters. For this reason, he began to increasingly appeal to their interests, pardoning their debts and placing favored officials in positions of power in São Paulo and Minas Gerais. He increasingly expressed nationalist anti-leftist sentiments, forgetting that he had essentially come to power through a platform to end the dominance of the landowner elites.

The ambiguity of his stances and the lack of cohesion that usually characterizes the actions of populist leaders manifested itself in the 1934 Constitution, adopted after extensive work by the National Constituent Assembly. The biggest political changes included the implementation of secret ballot voting and the extension of suffrage to women. It also granted extensive rights to the government to regulate the economy. Brazilian resources were nationalized, and a corporatist system was set up, promoting cooperation between the largest interest groups inside the country (not only business corporations).

Vargas' regime was showing great resemblance to some of the ultra-nationalist and fascist regimes gaining prominence in contemporary Europe, namely those of Benito Mussolini in Italy and Adolf Hitler in Germany. Vargas began to adopt increasingly fascist rhetoric after the Communist uprising of November 1935 in Recife and Rio, which was quickly suppressed by government forces. The president began to blame the leftist groups for their continued efforts to destabilize the Brazilian state. The uprising had essentially provided Vargas with a new scapegoat.

Knowing that he would be barred from re-election in 1938, he addressed the nation in November 1937 with a radio speech, informing the country of a Communist plot to overthrow the government. According to him, radical leftist groups had devised the "Cohen Plan" with which they wanted to establish a Communist dictatorship in the country. However, no such conspiracy existed. The president had made it up to justify some of the measures he would take next, seemingly to defend the country from the revolutionaries. Thus, following his speech, Vargas proceeded to declare a state of emergency and dissolve the Congress. He quickly announced a new constitution that granted the president virtually unlimited powers and contained anti-communist, nationalist rhetoric.

So began a new era in the history of Brazil deemed *Estado Novo*, or the "New State," also referred to as the Third Brazilian Republic. For the next eight years, Vargas essentially acted as the dictator of the country, justifying his stay in power by scapegoating leftist groups and cracking down on whoever dared to express their opposition. Brazil was turned into a police state, with the army Vargas' main ally in maintaining the regime.

Political and civil society opponents, critics of the regime, suspected dissenters, and activists were imprisoned and tried in tribunals set up by the regime to pursue its own ends. All political parties were dissolved by a presidential decree, including the fascist Integralist Party, which had until that point been the main political ally of Vargas against the Communists. Censorship laws were put in place and enforced by the regime. Economic measures were taken to push industrialization and quell any discontented sentiments the public might have against the dictator. State companies were created to better control Brazilian resources.

With the outbreak of World War II, Vargas proceeded to justify his further stay in power based on the tense international situation. Brazil was formally neutral at first, though Vargas' efforts at forming close ties with the United States meant that the country provided valuable wartime materials to the Allies, such as rubber and iron. The rubber industry, based around the Amazon basin, was especially developed, as the Axis powers had taken over the largest rubber reserves in Southeast Asia.

Only in 1942, after its merchant ships were sunk by German submarines, did Brazil join the war on the side of the Allies. The Brazilian Expeditionary Force was sent to Europe, achieving great prestige for the Brazilians despite its lack of training and adequate equipment compared to other Allied nations. In turn, the United States granted Brazil land-lease grants and air support throughout the war, which helped Vargas sustain his position until 1945.

The Fourth Brazilian Republic

Ironically, the success of the Brazilian Expeditionary Force (BEF) was one of the factors in the decline of Vargas' authority by the end of 1945. With international tensions dying down and the war ending, pressure against Vargas from inside the country began to increase. Returning BEF soldiers were put under surveillance by the government, which feared they might emerge as leaders of a popular movement against Vargas.

These fears materialized in another non-violent military coup in late October 1945, which succeeded in deposing Vargas and ending the Estado Novo. Led by several army officers, the coup followed the fixing of the presidential elections on December 2 of the same year. Crucially, Vargas had announced plans to draw up a new constitution and had declared his intent to run. In fact, this might have been the reason he wished to change the constitution, as the previous iterations did not allow for the acting president to run immediately for a second term. With pressure from the public mounting and many feeling threatened by the idea that Vargas could stay in power, the coup d'état of October 29 was organized. Vargas was forced to resign, though the former dictator remained active in Brazilian politics.

In the elections held in December of the same year, Eurico Dutra, the Minister of War during Vargas' regime, emerged victorious with about 55 percent of the popular vote. He was from the same center-right Social Democratic Party founded by Vargas (the other being the Brazilian Labor Party) and had defeated the candidates from the conservative National Democratic Union and the Brazilian Communist Party.

A new constitution was established the very next year, marking the return of the country to democratic rule and the beginning of the Fourth Brazilian Republic. The constitution repealed the authoritarian measures of 1937 and aimed to restrict the powers of the president to avoid the rise of another Vargas. Presidential terms were fixed at five years instead of four, and greater autonomy was granted to the Brazilian states. All in all, the presidency of Eurico Dutra marked a relatively peaceful and stable five years. During this time, the government forged closer relations with the United States and modestly invested in key sectors of the Brazilian economy.

Interestingly, despite his deposition, Getúlio Vargas still maintained a high level of popularity among a certain base of supporters. He managed to become a senator by amassing popular support from Rio Grande do Sul and São Paulo and served during the presidency of Dutra. Even more importantly, the 1950 elections would mark Vargas' return as a presidential candidate from his populist Brazilian Labor Party and, ultimately, his victory in the elections with 48 percent of the national vote.

Vargas was inaugurated for his second term in January 1951, and his return as the president marked one of the most perplexing periods during the Fourth Republic. Vargas had technically defeated his opponents during the elections, though the number of votes he and his party had received was not enough to put him back in the position he had enjoyed in the 1930s. The party did not hold a majority in the National Congress, and the reduced powers of the president outlined in the new constitution meant that Vargas did not have free reign over the policies adopted during his second term. Still, the president-elect relied on populist rhetoric to stir up nationalist sentiments in the Brazilian public and succeeded in reinstating some of his old political allies to positions of power.

The Brazilian economy was still struggling to keep up with modernization, and the government was torn between adopting a neoliberal or interventionist stance. Some of the measures taken during Vargas' second presidency included doubling the minimum wage—a radical policy that only contributed to the rising inflation. Government spending was still too high, resulting in budget deficits and an increase in the national debt. Perhaps the most important decision of the government was the creation of a national petroleum company, Petrobras, to better develop the country's oil reserves.

Meanwhile, Vargas' main opponents continued to voice their concerns over his return as the president. This time, thanks to the existence of a free press and freedom of expression—two things not available to the critics during Vargas' dictatorship—their disapproval of the government reached new highs. Members of Vargas' administration were increasingly criticized, and some were dismissed from office by 1954.

The main anti-Vargas opposition party—the National Democratic Union—was joined by some members of the military in its critical remarks against the president. This created the sense that another conspiracy was brewing, putting further pressure on Vargas.

In early August 1954, there was an attempted murder of an opposition journalist and a vocal critic of Vargas, Carlos Lacerda. Lacerda had begun a campaign to run for the Chamber of Deputies and was frequently threatened, forcing him to hire a group of bodyguards. Ultimately, he survived the attack, but one of his bodyguards (a former air force officer) was killed, and another was wounded. The news of the attempted assassination soon hit national headlines, and after an investigation, one of Vargas' personal guards, Gregório Fortunado, was identified as the man who had ordered the assassination.

This set off another wave of public protests against Vargas and his administration, which was accused of widespread corruption. The public was joined by members of the military, who expressed their wish for Vargas' resignation. Following the scandal, President Vargas committed suicide in the presidential palace on August 24, fearing that a military coup against him was imminent. He left behind a letter in which he claimed that he had done everything for Brazil.

After an interim period during which three different individuals were chosen to fulfill the duties of the president, the former Governor of Minas Gerais, Juscelino Kubitschek de Oliveira, clinched a victory in the presidential elections held in October 1955. His ascendency marked the beginning of the end of the Fourth Brazilian Republic, which lasted until 1964.

Kubitschek, who became president with just over one-third of the total votes, was one of the most ambitious figures in the history of twentieth-century Brazil. His "Fifty Years in Five" program was an extensive plan to push for reforms in a wide range of social, economic, and political aspects of Brazilian life. This included proposed changes to such important fields as the country's infrastructure, communication and transport systems, energy sector, and education. In short, he wanted to rapidly industrialize the country, and his policies were a testament to his intentions. The government took over and began investing in industries such as hydroelectric power production and iron

Official presidential portrait of Joscelino Kubitschek.[10]

and coal mining and expanded its control over the petroleum industry.

Perhaps the most evident legacy of Kubitschek's administration was the construction of a new capital city—Brasilia—which was designed by prominent Brazilian architect Oscar Niemeyer. Strategically constructed nearly 600 miles west of Rio de Janeiro in an underdeveloped part of the country, Brasilia was supposed to attract a large number of inhabitants and accelerate the growth of the region.

Kubitschek's administration and decisions were heavily criticized, however. This was mainly because the state greatly increased its expenditures and added to its national debt by borrowing from foreign sources. By the end of his term, Brazil's debt had increased to 300 million USD, more than a threefold increase from 1956. Much like his predecessors, the president was criticized for neglecting the welfare of the lower strata of Brazilian society in favor of his goals to accelerate economic growth. Though the influx of foreign capital did result in the growth of several national industries, it has also increased domestic wealth inequality. Living standards remained horrible for many Brazilians in the rural areas as well as in the urban centers. This resulted in Kubitschek's support plummeting by the end of his tenure as president, and he was replaced after the 1960 elections by Jânio Quadros, a candidate from Vargas' old National Labor Party.

An extremely popular candidate at the time of his election, Quadros assumed the office of the president in 1961 and emerged as a vocal critic of the measures undertaken during the previous administration. He adopted the image of a politician with a desire to root out the widespread corruption in Brazilian politics but was unable to implement effective policies to address the problems faced by Brazil. This is why Quadros' presidency was marked by a subtle return of populism.

For instance, the president proceeded to ban gambling in the country, justifying his decision by saying that it was one of the main causes of inflation. The president also adopted a controversial foreign policy initiative by reestablishing diplomatic relations with the socialist and Communist nation of Cuba, seemingly to make Brazil a neutral nation during the Cold War.

We must remember that the United States had been Brazil's closest international ally before these developments, with intentions to deepen the relationship expressed early on by both sides. It was during Quadros' tenure as president that this relationship took a first hit. With it came a dissatisfied National Congress. Quadros lost his support and eventually resigned in August 1961, just five months after taking office.

Chapter Six – The Birth of Modern Brazil

The Coup of 1964

Jânio Quadros' resignation was an unexpected decision. Many have identified it as a move the president had hoped would cause the public to demonstrate its support toward him and make him return to power. No such support materialized, however. Instead, the National Congress recalled Vice President João Goulart from his trip to China to assume the office. (The vice president's mission was to normalize relations with the Communist nation, per Quadros' policy.)

Certain prominent individuals, however—mostly military officers—were against Goulart, believing he was himself a Communist and therefore an enemy of Brazil. The military ministers of the navy, army, and the air force vetoed Goulart's accession and wanted to hold new elections. Still, their decision did not amass widespread public support, and the Congress launched the Legality Campaign to ensure that Goulart became president.

Led by several state governors, military officers, and constitutionalist legislators, the campaigners believed that the ministers' decision to veto Goulart violated the constitution. Members of the public and parts of the army were mobilized, but, fortunately, no armed confrontation took place between the two groups.

Instead, they reached a compromise. Goulart was sworn in as a temporary replacement for Quadros but with limited powers that were implemented after changes were made to the constitution. Instead of the president, the prime minister assumed executive powers. This system lasted until early January of 1963 when voters took to the polls in a national referendum and voted in favor of reversing the amendments made to the constitution. This meant the parliamentarian system was abandoned, amendments were repealed, and pre-1961 powers were returned to President Goulart.

Nevertheless, it was obvious by this time that the political tensions in the country had not faded away. Quadros' resignation had caused massive polarization between the different groups in Brazil. Throughout the early 1960s, strikes and mass protests were common in the largest Brazilian cities, but little was done to address the problems faced by many Brazilians.

Once his powers were increased, Goulart tried to push for left-leaning reforms, such as more active involvement of the state in the nation's economy and land redistribution. In theory, these reforms would have diminished the power of some of the wealthiest landowners who still dominated the Brazilian social and political sphere. The president's critics increasingly thought of him as a Communist, and his support in the National Congress began to wane.

Amidst the international crises that were caused by the Cold War, such measures also drew the interest of the United States, which saw itself as the main enemy of the spread of Communism around the world. American-Brazilian relations continued to deteriorate as President Goulart refused to stop implementing his measures. Meanwhile, anti-Goulart movements began to gain prominence, and the instability and polarization that existed inside the country resulted in another conspiracy against the president, supported by the United States.

So was launched the military coup d'état of March 31, 1964, which succeeded in deposing Goulart. The uprising began after prominent members of the military joined anti-Goulart protests that had broken out in Minas Gerais. Among the chief leaders were Humberto Castelo Branco, who ultimately became the new president after Goulart was overthrown. Members of the National Congress also supported the insurrection, having secretly communicated with the US State Department for support against the seemingly Communist Goulart.

With "Operation Brother Sam," the US Air Force and US Navy had been mobilized to transport supplies to the coup's instigators and were ready to arrive in Brazil. However, their involvement in the coup was not necessary, as pro-Goulart groups could not to provide resistance to the coup. Rebel troops proceeded to occupy key positions in Rio de Janeiro and São Paulo, convincing more and more soldiers to join their cause. Goulart fled into exile to Uruguay the very same day, and by April 2, he was no longer able to mount resistance.

Dictatorship in Brazil

The new regime was maintained in Brazil for the next twenty-one years, marking a transformative period for the country amidst a turbulent international climate. The instigators of the coup instantly began implementing measures aimed at strengthening and legitimizing the new regime. Instead of repealing the 1946 Constitution, the military government adopted extra-legal decrees, the Institutional Acts. These acts gave the leaders of the coup political leverage and the self-ascribed authority to act beyond the borders of the constitution. The first of such acts was issued on April 9, 1964, greatly increasing the powers of the president. Two days later, the National Congress elected General Castelo Branco to serve as president for the remainder of the term of former President Goulart.

Castelo Branco's tenure as president kicked off relatively calmly. The first dictatorial measures he took came only in October 1965 with the adoption of the Second Institutional Act. With this decree, the executive was once again granted virtually unlimited powers, while those of the judiciary and the legislative branches were greatly reduced. The president could essentially choose favored lawmakers and governors, as well as dismiss them from office if he saw fit. Deputies critical of the regime, as well as left-leaning members of the National Congress, were thus purged, and many former military officers were given ministerial positions. Castelo Branco and his government then proceeded to outlaw all but two political parties: the National Renewal Alliance (ARENA)—a far-right party backed by the ruling government—and the Brazilian Democratic Movement, which constituted the "centrist" opposition.

A new constitution was also written in 1967, reaffirming the supremacy of the president and the Brazilian Armed Forces as his right-hand institution. The president could propose legislation to the National Congress, which had thirty days to review it. If there was no clear response from the Congress during the thirty days, the proposed decrees would automatically become laws. State autonomies were reduced, and fundamental freedoms of assembly, for example, were restricted. The competencies of the police were also increased; those suspected of being criminals could be freely imprisoned and tried in courts. Another important change impacted the election of the president and state governors. The elections were made indirect: the National Congress chose the president, and state legislatures chose their governors. In actuality, these measures only gave more power to the government to perpetuate the regime and increase its powers. The country's name was also changed to the Federative Republic of Brazil.

Castelo Branco was replaced as president by one of the toughest anti-communist hard-liners of the military dictatorship, Artur da Costa e Silva. His time in office was marked by the adoption of more authoritarian and nationalist measures that were often the subject of public protest.

The government proceeded to censor the Brazilian media, which had emerged as one of the most vocal critics of the regime despite supporting the deposition of Goulart in prior years. Special state bodies were created to oversee the implementation and enforcement of censorship laws, acting under the Ministry of Justice. Virtually all fields of media and communications, including radio, television, newspaper, and cultural spheres like theater or music, were censored by the government starting in 1968, leading to the creation of a "black market" for information transmission. These changes were made possible through several Institutional Acts. During this time, these decrees became a staple mechanism for increasing the power of the military dictatorship and overcoming the barriers created by the constitution.

It was also during this time that the systematic use of violence became another staple of the military dictatorship. The government essentially gave the police free reign to crack down on non-sympathetic members of the public. The state had engaged in similar activities during Vargas' presidency, but this time the scope of police brutality reached new highs, and the methods of torture were especially brutal. Those suspected of being members of secret left-wing organizations or protest movement organizers were imprisoned and tortured. This was especially the case during the first few years of the military dictatorship when protests by students, left-wing groups, artists, and civil society members were more common. Clashes with the riot police would result in hundreds of deaths and injuries and even more imprisonments.

To make them more effective, Brazilian police and members of the army were specially trained by US and UK intelligence experts who specialized in torture methods. The troubled legacy of the human rights abuses during the Silva regime lives on in Brazil, and many efforts have been made since the 1980s to root out the systematic brutal practices of the dictatorship.

Silva's presidency was cut short in August 1969 when he suffered a cerebral thrombosis that incapacitated him. Instead of Vice President Pedro Aleixo taking over, however, a military junta comprised of three generals assumed control of the country and decreed several Institutional Acts to legitimize itself.

The leaders of the junta justified their decision by the fact that the National Congress was still in recess. They wished to proceed by sharing the duties of the president among the three, but this proved impossible due to protests from the political and public spheres. Thus, a new election date was set in late October. Of course, a National Renewal Alliance candidate—Emílio Garrastazu Médici—prevailed, becoming the next president of the country in late 1969.

The repressive measures of Silva's presidency were taken to new highs during Médici's tenure as the government continued to exercise extensive control over public life. In general, the regime continued to crack down on political dissidents and vocal critics of the government. It restricted individual freedoms, censored the press, and adopted an increasingly nationalist and anti-leftist rhetoric.

However, the oppressiveness of Médici's term was complemented by great efforts to boost the nation's economy, which resulted in the "Brazilian Miracle," to the surprise of many domestic and international observers. Government policies resulted in the magnificent average annual growth of 11.2 percent of the country's GDP, and inflation rates were kept stable until late 1973. Thanks to the plan devised by a group of technocrat economists led by Antônio Delfim Netto, Brazil managed to attract foreign investors and boost domestic production in industries such as car manufacturing. The output of the national economy was diversified, and coffee was no longer the main export of the country, with its share dropping to about 15 percent in the first half of the 1970s.

The Brazilian Miracle had been partially due to the favorable international financial situation, which made it easier for Brazil to borrow money from overseas sources. Though the country's total GDP increased, there were also clear winners and losers of the economic policies, which favored the accumulation of capital in the hands of the wealthiest members of society. The state proceeded to drop many of its social welfare programs, which hit the lower social strata the worst. Additionally, the oil crisis of 1973 dealt a massive blow to the Brazilian economy, as petroleum had been among the most imported resources for the country.

By the end of Médici's term, the socio-economic situation in Brazil was very contradictory. The country was on an upward industrialization course with one of the worst qualities of life for the large majority of its society.

Abertura

The election of Ernesto Beckmann Geisel as president in 1974 is usually associated in Brazilian history with the beginning of liberalization and the gradual transition away from a fully authoritarian dictatorship. This time has become known as the period of "political opening" or *abertura*, but it is not to be confused with the era of radical changes that brought about the instant re-democratization of Brazil. In fact, Geisel was elected according to the established "tradition" of the military regime since 1964—nominated by the leadership of the armed forces and elected without any real opposition. He had been chosen because of his army credentials, close connections to the regime since the time of Castelo Branco, and the influence of his brother, who was the Minister of War. Nobody foresaw at the time that his tenure would begin a gradual process of liberalization that would continue for the next ten years.

His moderate leanings were well-known inside ARENA, and to be sure, there was some opposition against him from the most ardent supporters of the dictatorial regime. However, it is not easy to pinpoint the reasons behind the gradual liberalization program he adopted during his presidency.

One of the main reasons might have been the crisis Brazil had found itself in since 1973, caused by the fluctuation of international oil prices. The roots of this problem could be traced back to the strict military hierarchy imposed. Geisel thought that it would be better for Brazil in the long term to slowly separate the military from governmental affairs. Although this could not be done instantly for obvious reasons, his administration ultimately was responsible for at least creating an atmosphere that allowed the opposition to voice its concerns.

Yet, many of the measures of the *abertura* were followed by equally conservative and authoritarian crackdowns, some reminiscent of Médici's rule. For instance, opposition parties were allowed to use radio and television during their campaigns for the state legislature elections that were held in November 1974. The Brazilian Democratic Movement (MDB) was thus able to finally gain more representation in regional legislatures. However, this was followed by a crackdown on the Communist Party and press censorship measures of 1975, which were in keeping with the strong anti-communist stance of the military regime.

In short, what Geisel correctly recognized was the fact that Brazil's political system was not sustainable and changes could only be imposed from positions of power. The 1974 state legislature elections went a long way to revitalize the opposition movement, and subsequent elections were all held in a similarly free manner. This resulted in the MDB winning even more seats in the National Congress in 1976. For the first time, this may have threatened the position of ARENA. Geisel was thus quick to utilize the powers granted to him by the Fifth Institutional Act to dissolve the Congress in 1977 and create structures that guaranteed the accession of his desired successor. This approach of allowing for gradual democratizing advances and then countering them with authoritarian measures became a staple of his presidency.

Ultimately, Geisel's approach gave many people who had been disenchanted with Brazilian leadership a sense of hope and the desire to take to the streets. Thus came the labor strike movements of the greater São Paulo area in 1978, the first organized strikes after the repressive policies of the government. Organized by the left-wing parties and led by then-activist and eventual president Luiz Inácio Lula da Silva, workers began to demand wage increases and better conditions. Up to half a million people took to the streets, and the government ultimately acquiesced to their demands.

All these developments added up. By the end of his term, President Geisel had effectively ended press censorship, repealed the Institutional Acts that granted the president virtually limitless powers, and revived the political opposition.

Geisel's presidency also saw significant shifts in the direction of Brazilian economic and foreign policy. Though the president continued to borrow heavily to deal with the trade deficit and inflation, many of his measures were directed at making Brazil less dependent on imports in the long term. The government renewed heavy investments into the state's infrastructural and communication projects, including in rural and underdeveloped areas that had previously been neglected. Notably, he supported the diversification of the Brazilian energy sector and the country's dependence on oil imports by encouraging the development of the ethanol production industry.

The technocratic group of economists responsible for the neoliberal policies during the Brazilian Miracle was dismissed, and the country adopted a foreign policy that complemented the economic changes. For instance, though the United States remained a strong trade partner, Brazil began to forge closer ties with European and Asian nations. Geisel managed to strike a deal with West Germany worth roughly ten billion USD, financing the construction of eight nuclear reactors in the country, following his intention to diversify the energy sector.

Nuclear power was a sustainable and, in the long-term, cheap solution to Brazil's dependence on oil. Brazil's new international partners and reduced reliance on the United States alarmed Washington, which responded by increasing its criticism of the Brazilian regime's continued human rights violations. Ultimately, this put more pressure on Geisel and his successor, João Figueiredo, to tone down the government's repressive measures against political dissidents and opponents.

Democratization

João Figueiredo, who assumed the office of president in March 1979, continued the political liberalization begun by Geisel. Interestingly, Figueiredo had been a long-standing member of the military regime, even serving as the head of the National Intelligence Bureau and overseeing many of the violent practices of the regime during the 1970s.

Figueiredo was sworn in while Brazil was experiencing yet another economic crisis caused by the instability of the global market, with inflation reaching as high as 110 percent in 1980. The crisis hit the lowest sectors of Brazilian society the hardest, who continued to organize mass demonstrations against the government. The government could not deal with these domestic problems and had to ask the International Monetary Fund for a bailout in 1983. After rigorous negotiations, the IMF loaned Brazil a huge sum of money at a high interest rate. But the IMF was upset when Figueiredo's administration did not reduce spending to uphold its part of the deal. Though the country's GDP technically continued to grow during his presidency, so did inflation, which had doubled to about 223 percent by 1984.

One of the most important policies of Figueiredo's administration—one that perhaps played the biggest part in re-democratizing the country—was the amnesty law for political exiles and dissidents who had been previously persecuted by the military government. The amnesty law was adopted despite harsh criticism from several prominent hard-liner army officials, who wished to maintain the status quo. Occupying important positions in the government, they perhaps feared they would be punished for their crimes if they gave up power. Importantly, in December 1979, Figueiredo decided to abolish the two-party system with the help of the National Congress. He forced them to reform their structures, thus allowing new parties to emerge. New social groups began to be formed that called for more liberalization and the end of military rule. These were mostly left-wing groups, a broad alliance ranging from moderate social democrats to more radical socialists who advocated for the proletariat's rise to power.

Forty-eight million Brazilians took to the polls for the 1982 midterm elections. For the first time since the 1960s, state governors and local legislature were elected by direct ballot. The opposition thus emerged victorious in the crucial southern states of Minas Gerais, Rio de Janeiro, and São Paulo, giving it much-needed motivation even though the Democratic Social Party (PDS), the successor to the regime's old ARENA, won a majority in both chambers of the National Congress.

The Workers' Party, or *Partido dos Trabalhadores* (PT), was among the most active opposition groups, and it began working with other political parties to create a unified front against the regime. It began advocating for direct presidential elections, something that could only be achieved by a two-thirds constitutional majority in the Congress. A respective constitutional amendment was drafted and put to the vote, but the PDS-dominated national legislature rejected it.

The 1985 elections proceeded in a volatile political climate. The existing disputes among the members of the regime resulted in unfavorable pre-election conditions. President Figueiredo had favored Colonel Mário Andreazza as his successor, who ultimately lost the nomination to former São Paulo Governor Paulo Maluf, supported by more conservative members of the PDS. This, ultimately, caused a split inside the party. Many members left the PDS, giving the upper hand to the opposition. This included José Sarney, the former president of ARENA and a long-time member of the ruling regime. Sarney became the new leader of the Liberal National Front, comprised of former PDS dissident members. He became a running mate of the opposition's Tancredo Neves, a veteran of Brazilian politics before the military dictatorship and the acting governor of Minas Gerais, who ran for the Brazilian Democratic Movement (MDB).

Together, the Neves-Sarney ballot emerged victorious in the 1985 presidential elections, accruing over 70 percent of the votes and decisively defeating the government's nominee, Paulo Maluf. It was a decisive defeat for the regime, which lost the presidential elections by 300 votes in the electoral college, only winning in two states. The twenty-one-year military dictatorship in Brazil thus ended, only the second instance in the history of Brazil when the sitting government transferred power peacefully to a new president. Unfortunately, there were additional hurdles for the opposition. Before he could be inaugurated into office in March, president-elect Neves fell ill and underwent an emergency operation in Brasilia. Sarney was inaugurated in his stead on March 15. Though this was supposed to be temporary, Neves' health continued to decline, leading to his death on April 21.

Neves was mourned by the public, who feared what could happen with the death of their new leader at such a critical moment. This sentiment was especially prominent because Vice President Sarney, who acted out Neves' term until 1990, was a former member of the old military dictatorship. However, these fears did not materialize. Sarney honored the promises he had made during their campaign and appointed ministers that Neves had favored.

Sarney's first year as president marked the legalization of all political parties, including the Brazilian Communist Party, which had long been outlawed from Brazilian politics. By then, however, it had lost its prestige and mass support, with most Brazilians happily supporting the moderate center-left PT. He followed it up with the ambitious Cruzado Plan—a set of economic measures to fight soaring inflation in the country, including price regulation. The plan, despite a brief period of initial success, ultimately failed, resulting in an increase in Brazil's trade deficit by 1987 and a shortage of supplies.

The following year, a new constitution finally ended the legitimized authoritarian practices of the military government. The new constitution reaffirmed personal and social liberties but was subject to criticism for its ambiguity in reorganizing the federalist system, which had been a staple of Brazilian democracy for a long time. Nevertheless, Sarney's accession as president marked the end of the more than a decade-long struggle to democratize in Brazil. In an international context, it was part of a large wave of democratization throughout the world. In Latin America, Brazil provided an example for the end of authoritarian regimes in Chile and Argentina, while the global democratization process culminated with the fall of the Soviet Union.

In 1989, Brazil had its first direct presidential elections since 1960. Fernando Collor de Mello from the National Reconstruction Party emerged victorious over PT's candidate, Luiz Inacio da Silva (Lula). He became the next president of the country with about thirty-six million votes from the public, while Lula amassed about thirty-one million. Collor won with a neoliberal platform that called for the reduction of government spending and continued to battle the country's severe economic difficulties throughout his term. Although he had been a vocal critic of the existing corruption in Brazilian politics, he was accused of partaking in corruption schemes during his presidency, leading to his impeachment by the Chamber of Deputies in 1992. When his case went up for discussion in the Senate, it became clear he would be convicted, impeached, and disqualified from running again for public office for a time. This prompted Collor to resign from his position, and Vice President Itamar Franco to become acting president for the next two years.

Since the reestablishment of democracy, Brazil has struggled to keep up with the rapidly modernizing world and a globalized society. To this day, the country is plagued with one of the most unequal wealth and income distributions in the world. This resulted in Lula becoming the first ever left-wing president of Brazil in 2002 and his subsequent reelection in 2006, as Brazil experimented with social democracy.

The PT emerged victorious in the 2010 elections as well, leading to the election of the nation's first female president—Dilma Rousseff. She was also reelected in 2014 but was impeached following her involvement in corruption scandals and the increased spending that characterized her tenure as president. "Operation Car Wash"—the investigation that ultimately uncovered the widespread corruption in which many of Brazil's former top politicians were actively involved—was a hit to the prestige of the PT.

The impeachment of Rousseff led to the election of Jair Bolsonaro in 2018, a far-right populist leader from the Social Liberal Party. Bolsonaro's accession as president marked the return of populism to Brazil, part of a wider tendency for world democracies to turn to right-wing populist leaders. Despite his victory, Bolsonaro's policies were widely unpopular both domestically and internationally, especially as his term coincided with the COVID pandemic. He did not effectively deal with the problems caused by the pandemic, including a severe economic crisis, and was also accused of anti-vaccine propaganda campaigns that worsened public health during the most pressing time for the country. Ultimately, his presidency was also marked with several major scandals.

In the 2022 presidential elections, the two-time former president Lula managed to clinch elections with just 50.90 percent of the total votes, making it the closest in the country's history.

Conclusion

Once an unknown promised land on the edge of the known world, Brazil now stands as the fifth largest country in the world by area and the seventh largest in population. It is also the eleventh largest economy with a total national GDP of nearly two trillion USD. Since its discovery and colonization, Brazil has certainly come a long way to its current position. Its journey from pre-colonial times to the present is like that of many other Latin American nations. Still, there is an aura of uniqueness when it comes to Brazil, especially compared to other post-colonial countries on the continent.

The history of Brazil is a history of the strong personalities who dominated the political landscape of the country since the colonial era. Their interests and conflicts shaped the social structures that are still prevalent today and influence not only how the world perceives Brazil, but also how Brazilians perceive themselves. And yet, one thing that perhaps best characterizes Brazilian history is the struggle of the people. Often neglected for the interests of their leaders, they nevertheless continued to fight for their rights, fundamental freedoms, and prosperity— which they deserved, above all.

It is fascinating to see that Brazil has become one of the most diverse countries in the world, with a unique culture that combines the best of the many different peoples that inhabit it. Brazil is known for its hospitality and exciting way of life, which captivates visitors to this day.

The dark memory of oppression, including the practice of slavery, which lasted until the late nineteenth century and cost the lives of millions of innocent people, lives on today. Inequality between the different parts of society can clearly be observed by those who witness the favelas in Rio, and it is only after closely examining the history of the country that the structural reasons behind these inequalities can be identified.

It is Brazilian history that can provide explanations and even solutions to many of the deeply rooted systemic problems that plague Brazil to this day. The aim of this book was to highlight the key developments where these answers can be found and provide insight to readers of all ages and tastes into the captivating history of such a remarkable country as Brazil.

If you enjoyed this book, a review on Amazon would be greatly appreciated because it would mean a lot to hear from you.

To leave a review:

1. Open your camera app.
2. Point your mobile device at the **QR** code.
3. The review page will appear in your web browser.

Thanks for your support!

Here's another book by Enthralling History that you might like

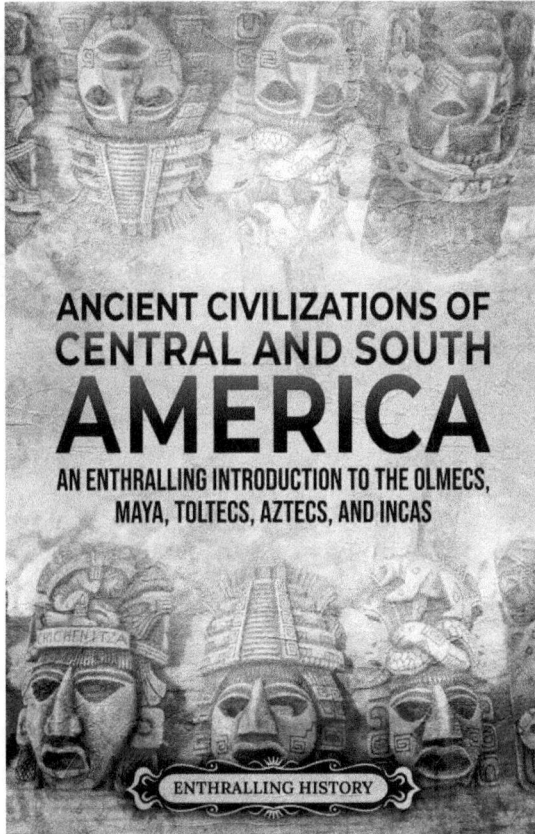

ANCIENT CIVILIZATIONS OF
CENTRAL AND SOUTH
AMERICA
AN ENTHRALLING INTRODUCTION TO THE OLMECS,
MAYA, TOLTECS, AZTECS, AND INCAS

ENTHRALLING HISTORY

Free limited time bonus

We forget 90% of everything
that we've read in 7 days...

Get the free printable pdf summary of
the book you've read AND much, much
more... shhhh...

Enter Your Most Frequently Used Email to Get Started

**DOWNLOAD FREE PDF
SUMMARY**

© Enthralling History

Stop for a moment. We have a free bonus set up for you. The problem is this: we forget 90% of everything that we read after 7 days. Crazy fact, right? Here's the solution: we've created a printable, 1-page pdf summary for this book that you're reading now. All you have to do to get your free pdf summary is to go to the following website: **https://livetolearn.lpages.co/enthrallinghistory/**

Or, Scan the QR code!

Once you do, it will be intuitive. Enjoy, and thank you!

Sources

1. Bethell, Leslie. "Populism in Brazil." In *Brazil: Essays on History and Politics*, 175–194. University of London Press, 2018. http://www.jstor.org/stable/j.ctv51309x.10

2. Bethell, Leslie. "The Decline and Fall of Slavery in Brazil (1850–88)." In *Brazil: Essays on History and Politics*, 113–144. University of London Press, 2018. http://www.jstor.org/stable/j.ctv51309x.8

3. Bethell, Leslie. "The Long Road to Democracy in Brazil." In *Brazil: Essays on History and Politics*,147–174. University of London Press, 2018. http://www.jstor.org/stable/j.ctv51309x.9

4. Bethell, Leslie, ed. *Colonial Brazil*. Cambridge University Press, 1987.

5. Burns, E. Bradford, Momsen, Richard P., Martins, Luciano, James, Preston E., and Schneider, Ronald Milton. "Brazil." *Encyclopedia Britannica*, August 28, 2024. https://www.britannica.com/place/Brazil

6. Fausto, B., and Fausto, S. *A Concise History of Brazil*. Cambridge University Press, 2014.

7. Martin, Percy Alvin. "Slavery and Abolition in Brazil." *The Hispanic American Historical Review* 13, no. 2 (1933): 151–196. https://doi.org/10.2307/2506690

8. Meade, T. A. *A Brief History of Brazil*. Infobase Publishing, 2010.

9. Newitt, M. *A History of Portuguese Overseas Expansion 1400-1668*. Routledge, 2004.

10. Putnam, Samuel. "Vargas Dictatorship in Brazil." *Science & Society* 5, no. 2 (1941): 97–116. http://www.jstor.org/stable/40399384

11. Teresa P. R. Caldeira, & Holston, J. "Democracy and Violence in Brazil." *Comparative Studies in Society and History* 41, no. 4 (1999): 691–729. http://www.jstor.org/stable/179426

Image Sources

[1] https://commons.wikimedia.org/wiki/File:Henry_the_Navigator1.jpg

[2] https://commons.wikimedia.org/wiki/File:Capitanias.jpg

[3] https://commons.wikimedia.org/wiki/File:Jesus,_Benedito_Calixto_de_-_Domingos_Jorge_Velho_e_o_Loco-tenente_Ant%C3%B4nio_F._de_Abreu.jpg

[4] https://commons.wikimedia.org/wiki/File:Bandeira_da_Inconfid%C3%AAncia_1789_Os_Inconfidentes.jpg

[5] https://commons.wikimedia.org/wiki/File:Retrato_de_D._Jo%C3%A3o_VI,_Rei_de_Portugal.jpg

[6] . https://commons.wikimedia.org/wiki/File:DpedroI-brasil-full.jpg

[7] https://en.wikipedia.org/wiki/File:Pedro_II_of_Brazil_-_Brady-Handy.jpg

[8] https://commons.wikimedia.org/wiki/File:Deodoro_da_Fonseca_(1889).jpg

[9] https://commons.wikimedia.org/wiki/File:Getulio_Vargas_(1930).jpg

[10] https://commons.wikimedia.org/wiki/File:Juscelino.jpg

www.ingramcontent.com/pod-product-compliance
Lightning Source LLC
LaVergne TN
LVHW051749080426
835511LV00018B/3279